GREAT ARTISTS OF THE WESTERN WORLD

The
Old Masters

GREAT ARTISTS OF THE WESTERN WORLD

The Old Masters

Peter Paul Rubens

—❧—

Frans Hals

—❧—

Rembrandt van Rijn

—❧—

Johannes Vermeer

MARSHALL CAVENDISH · LONDON · NEW YORK · SYDNEY

Staff Credits

Editors	Clive Gregory LL B Sue Lyon BA (Honours)	**Picture Researchers**	Vanessa Fletcher BA (Honours) Flavia Howard BA (Honours) Jessica Johnson BA
Art Editors	Kate Sprawson BA (Honours) Keith Vollans LSIAD		
Deputy Editor	John Kirkwood B Sc (Honours)	**Production Controllers**	Steve Roberts Alan Stewart BSc
Sub-editors	Caroline Bugler BA (Honours), MA Sue Churchill BA (Honours) Alison Cole BA, M Phil Jenny Mohammadi Nigel Rodgers BA (Honours), MA Penny Smith Will Steeds BA (Honours), MA	**Secretary**	Lynn Smail
		Publisher	Terry Waters Grad IOP
		Editorial Director	Maggi McCormick
		Production Executive	Robert Paulley B Sc
Designers	Stuart John Julie Stanniland	**Consultant and Authenticator**	Sharon Fermor BA (Honours) Lecturer in the Extra-Mural Department of London University and Lecturer in Art History at Sussex University

Reference Edition Published 1990

Published by Marshall Cavendish Corporation
147 West Merrick Road
Freeport, Long Island
N.Y. 11520

Typeset by Litho Link Ltd., Welshpool
Printed and Bound in Singapore by
Times Offset Private Ltd.

Library of Congress Cataloging-in-Publication Data

Main entry under title:

Great Artists of the Western World.

   Includes index.
   1. Artists – Biography. I. Marshall Cavendish Corporation
N40.G77 1987   709'.2'2 [B]   86–23863
ISBN 0–86307–743–9

ISBN 0–86307–743–9 (set)
     0–86307–746–3 (vol)

Preface

Looking at pictures can be one of the greatest pleasures that life has to offer. Note, however, those two words 'can be'; all too many of us remember all too clearly those grim afternoons of childhood when we were dragged, bored to tears and complaining bitterly, through room after room of Italian primitives by well-meaning relations or tight-lipped teachers. It was enough to put one off pictures for life – which, for some of us, was exactly what it did.

For if gallery-going is to be the fun it should be, certain conditions must be fulfilled. First, the pictures we are to see must be good pictures. Not necessarily great pictures – even a few of these can be daunting, while too many at a time may prove dangerously indigestible. But they must be well-painted, by good artists who know precisely both the effect they want to achieve and how best to achieve it. Second, we must limit ourselves as to quantity. Three rooms – four at the most – of the average gallery are more than enough for one day, and for best results we should always leave while we are still fresh, well before satiety sets in. Now I am well aware that this is a counsel of perfection: sometimes, in the case of a visiting exhibition or, perhaps, when we are in a foreign city with only a day to spare, we shall have no choice but to grit our teeth and stagger on to the end. But we shall not enjoy ourselves quite so much, nor will the pictures remain so long or so clearly in our memory.

The third condition is all-important: we must know something about the painters whose work we are looking at. And this is where this magnificent series of volumes – one of which you now hold in your hands – can make all the difference. No painting is an island: it must, if it is to be worth a moment's attention, express something of the personality of its painter. And that painter, however individual a genius, cannot but reflect the country, style and period, together with the views and attitudes of the people among whom he or she was born and bred. Even a superficial understanding of these things will illuminate a painting for us far better than any number of spotlights, and if in addition we have learnt something about the artist as a person – life and loves, character and beliefs, friends and patrons, and the places to which he or she travelled – the interest and pleasure that the work will give us will be multiplied a hundredfold.

Great Artists of the Western World will provide you with just such an insight into the life and work of some of the outstanding painters of Europe and America. The text is informative without ever becoming dry or academic, not limiting itself to the usual potted biographies but forever branching out into the contemporary world outside and beyond workshop or studio. The illustrations, in colour throughout, have been dispensed in almost reckless profusion. For those who, like me, revel in playing the Attribution Game – the object of which is to guess the painter of each picture before allowing one's eye to drop to the label – the little sections on 'Trademarks' are a particularly happy feature; but every aficionado will have particular preferences, and I doubt whether there is an art historian alive, however distinguished, who would not find some fascinating nugget of previously unknown information among the pages that follow.

This series, however, is not intended for art historians. It is designed for ordinary people like you and me – and for our older children – who are fully aware that the art galleries of the world constitute a virtually bottomless mine of potential enjoyment, and who are determined to extract as much benefit and advantage from it as they possibly can. All the volumes in this collection will enable us to do just that, expanding our knowledge not only of art itself but also of history, religion, mythology, philosophy, fashion, interior decoration, social customs and a thousand other subjects as well. So let us not simply leave them around, flipping idly through a few of their pages once in a while. Let us read them as they deserve to be read – and welcome a new dimension in our lives.

John Julius Norwich is a writer and broadcaster who has written histories of Venice and of Norman Sicily as well as several works on history, art and architecture. He has also made over twenty documentary films for television, including the recent Treasure Houses of Britain series which was widely acclaimed after repeated showings in the United States.

Lord Norwich is Chairman of the Venice in Peril Fund, and member of the Executive Committee of the British National Trust, an independently funded body established for the protection of places of historic interest and natural beauty.

John Julius Norwich

Contents

Introduction

Portraits opposite from left to right: National Gallery, London; Gift of John and Johanna Bass/Bass Museum of Art, Miami; Reproduced by Gracious Permission of Her Majesty the Queen/Royal Collection, London; The Michael Friedsam Collection, Bequest of Michael Friedsam, 1931/The Metropolitan Museum of Art.

Capitoline Museums, Rome

A hero in his time
(right) In Romulus and Remus and the She-Wolf – *the childhood of the legendary founders of Rome was a popular classical subject –* Rubens *displays all the mastery of composition and colour that led to his being compared by his contemporaries to one of the wonders of the world.*

The seventeenth century was the great age of the Baroque – a style which defies very precise definition, but which was characterized by dynamic movement, emotional rhetoric, flourish and ornateness. This manner of painting had its origins in Italy, in the work of artists such as Annibale Carracci and Caravaggio who sought to breathe new life into the conventions of religious and mythological painting. All the painters in this volume can be called Baroque artists, but each exemplifies different strands within the movement, and each possessed a highly individual vision.

In many ways, Rubens *is the Baroque artist* par excellence. *During his eight-year stay in Italy he studied closely the work of his Italian contemporaries and of the artists of the High Renaissance, and on his return he did much to integrate their ideas and techniques into his own work. Yet richness, vigour and emotional intensity can also be seen in the work of* Hals *and* Rembrandt, *linking them too with the art of southern Europe even though they never left the Netherlands.* Vermeer's *work is quieter altogether. The absolute antithesis of flourish and overstatement, his pictures stand as a testament to his ability to create subtle colour harmonies. However, his pursuit of painterly realism also links him with other Baroque artists such as* Caravaggio *and* Velásquez, *who were determined to record the details of the natural world as truthfully as possible.*

A Golden Age of Painting

During the seventeenth century, painting in the Low Countries enjoyed a golden era, and both Amsterdam and Antwerp became centres of a buoyant art market. Yet this followed nearly 80 years of civil war between the northern provinces (present-day Holland) and Flanders in the south (present-day Belgium).

Each nation in the divided Netherlands had its own distinctive cultural character, and some of the differences between the two countries are clearly apparent when the life and work of the Flemish artist Rubens is compared with those of his Dutch contemporaries: Rembrandt, Hals and Vermeer. Many of Rubens' large-scale canvases were commissions from the Catholic Church, which had the resources to fund ambitious projects. The destruction of many altarpieces during the fighting in Flanders had created a demand for new monumental paintings to adorn churches and cathedrals that Rubens and his fellow artists were only too happy to fulfil. In Flanders there was also extensive patronage from wealthy archdukes, governors, and members of the French and Spanish courts who wanted hunting scenes and mythological works, designs for tapestries and history paintings to adorn their palaces and castles. In the Dutch Republic, however, painters were forced to rely more on the open market, and their pictures were inevitably tailored to the demands of a more modest buyer, who tended to favour anecdotal scenes and interiors that were small enough to fit inside the bourgeois homes that they frequently depicted. State patronage was limited, and there were no commissions forthcoming from the Calvinist Church, which disapproved of religious imagery. On the other hand, civic institutions, such as guilds and militia companies, provided a constant demand for group portraits of the type that Hals made his speciality.

One of the Wonders of the World

These specific social circumstances go some way towards explaining why Rubens' work is so different in scope and intention from that of the Dutch painters in this volume. Yet his influence upon them should not be overlooked; both Hals and Rembrandt admired the animation and strong tonal contrasts in his pictures. Rubens' art is one of exuberance, colour and movement, with grandiose religious and mythological subject matter. His work marries the heroic conceptions of Italian painting with typically Flemish attention to detail, in compositions of tremendous dramatic force. This great achievement was universally recognized during his own lifetime.

Rubens was the leader of all around him and, although he cannot have had a great deal of spare time to devote to teaching, the example of his work was undoubtedly a revelation to a whole generation of Flemish artists. Indeed, it is hard to think of a single seventeenth-century Flemish painter who was not in some way influenced by his prodigious and ambitious output. The situation was very different in the Dutch Republic, where no one painter can be said to have exerted such a powerful influence over the artistic life of the nation. Instead, Holland had several masters and schools of painting, which were usually associated with individual towns. Rembrandt's astonishing achievement was widely acknowledged, but not every Dutch painter strove to emulate his style.

The artists
(below) From left to right: Rembrandt, a self-portrait at 34; the young Vermeer, a possible portrait; Rubens, a self-portrait in his mid-forties; Hals, a presumed self-portrait.

Holland's Supreme Genius

The emotional range and the deep human sympathy of Rembrandt's work set him apart from his contemporaries, and marked him out as one of the greatest painters that ever lived. Rembrandt painted a wide variety of subjects – portraits, mythological scenes, history pictures, religious works and landscapes – but his most potent source of inspiration came from the Bible rather than the Classical world. The artist was in fact resolutely anti-classical in his depiction of the human body, preferring to draw upon his observations of the people he saw around him every day, rather than on some remote ideal. Rembrandt's pictures fascinate the spectator by their paint surface. In the mature work, pigment is applied with astonishing confidence and mastery, the thick layers of paint building up a richly encrusted texture that perfectly conveys the tactile qualities of materials such as velvets, brocades and furs.

Master of the Fleeting Expression

The paintings of Frans Hals also display dazzling brushwork, but Hals never loaded on the paint in the manner of Rembrandt. Instead, he preferred to apply the pigment in rapid slashes, juxtaposing dabs of pure colour rather than blending them together. Hals is supposed to have told his pupils 'You must smear boldly; when you are settled in art, neatness will surely come by itself', and this robust approach lends enormous force and vitality to his pictures. Hals was the first Dutch painter to upset the conventions of portraiture and to experiment with informal and spontaneous-looking poses. He was a master of the fleeting expression, and he sometimes conveys the impression that his characters are reacting to events outside the picture space, directing their laughter or scorn at an unseen observer. These people are believable individuals whose features are never flattered or idealized.

Pure Pictorial Harmony

The men and women in Hals' portraits were prosperous Dutch burghers who wished to advertize their eminence and pride. Vermeer, however, chose to paint unassuming servants and housewives during their quiet moments at home playing the virginals, reading letters, or enjoying a subdued conversation. In contrast to the dash and swagger of Hals' pictures, Vermeer's paintings create a feeling of calm and stillness because of their studied equilibrium. In his compositions every element has

its precise place, and gentle scenes of domestic life are transformed into images of pure pictorial harmony, raising genre painting to a level that has never been surpassed. There is also an enigmatic quality about these pictures as they seem to challenge the spectator to piece together a narrative or meaning from various clues, and to invite speculation as to the nature of the thoughts in the minds of the characters depicted. Vermeer was passionately interested in light effects, and often his paintings experiment with illumination from one source – a window, for example – to explore the way that light falls upon individual objects.

It is true, of course, that all the painters represented in this volume shared this interest in capturing the fleeting moment in time; in portraying the specific rather than the general. Yet each painter pursued his ends in his individual way, and developed a unique style that set him apart from other, lesser talents. It is a tribute to their patrons taste that it was wide enough to embrace four very different artists.

Deutsche Fotothek Dresden

Dresden, Gemäldegalerie

Quiet calm
(left) Vermeer's Lady Reading a Letter at an Open Window *is a characteristically domestic subject for this artist who raised genre painting to heights unknown before or since.*

Royal Collection, London

Pietro Paolo Rubens

1577-1640

The greatest Flemish artist of the 17th century and one of the most prolific painters of all time, Rubens enjoyed a career of spectacular international success. From the time he returned from Italy at the age of 31 and set up in Antwerp he rapidly became the most sought-after painter in Europe. A brilliant manager as well as a brilliant artist, he ran a thriving workshop that poured out an unending flood of work.

Handsome, cultivated and a superb linguist, Rubens was also employed as a diplomat, and he was knighted by Charles I of England. However, although he lived his life on an international stage and was completely at home painting huge political allegories, there was also a very personal dimension to his art, which comes out in his paintings of his two beautiful wives and his beloved children.

11

The Artist-Diplomat

The crowded life of Rubens gives the impression of bustling, productive activity. Artist, diplomat and family man, he still found time to teach and run a busy and prolific workshop.

Ironically, the most famous painter of the Flemish School did not see Flanders until he was 10 years old, for he was born and grew up in Germany. His father, Jan Rubens, a lawyer, had fled from Antwerp in 1568 to escape religious persecution (though born a Catholic he was suspected of having Calvinist sympathies) and settled in Cologne. There he became secretary to Anna of Saxony, the wife of William the Silent, Prince of Orange. Jan and Anna had an affair and she became pregnant. But for the pleading of his wife Maria, a woman of resolute character, he would probably have paid with his life, instead, he was banished to the small town of Siegen in Westphalia, and there on 28 June 1577 Maria gave birth to the sixth of her seven children. The next

day was the feast of St Peter and St Paul, so the baby was named after them – Peeter Pauwel in Flemish, althought in later life he usually signed himself using the Italian form, Pietro Pauolo.

The family were allowed to move back to Cologne in the following year and in March 1587 Jan Rubens died. Soon afterwards the widowed Maria decided to move back to Antwerp with the three children who still formed part of the household – Peter Paul, his brother Philip, who was three years older, and a sister, Blandina, in her twenties (three had died young and the eldest son had left home). The boys had already had the beginnings of a good education from their learned father and were now sent to a Latin school run by a scholar called Rombout Verdonck.

Key dates

1577 born in Siegen, Germany

1587 returns with mother to Antwerp

1598 becomes master in Antwerp guild

1600 leaves for Italy

1603 visits Spain on first diplomatic mission

1609 appointed court painter to Albert and Isabella; marries Isabella Brant

1610-11 paints *Raising of the Cross*

1611-14 paints *Descent from the Cross*

1622-25 paints Marie de' Medici cycle

1626 death of his first wife

1628-9 visits Spain

1629-30 visits England; knighted by Charles I

1630 marries Hélène Fourment

1634 completes ceiling paintings for Whitehall Banqueting House

1635 buys Château de Steen

1640 dies in Antwerp

Home town
(above) Victims of Philip II's aggressively Catholic policy in the Netherlands, Rubens' family left their native Antwerp for Cologne, to return 20 years later on the death of the painter's father. After this, Rubens regarded the city as his base.

Cologne childhood
(right) Although born in Siegen in 1577, Rubens spent most of his first 10 years in Cologne. Despite the shadow cast by the continuing repercussions of his father's infidelity with Anna of Saxony, he was to always regard the city with affection.

Wallraf Richartz Museum, Cologne

British Museum, London

In 1590, however, Peter Paul's schooldays came to an end. His sister married then, and the need to provide a dowry emphasized how strained Maria's financial resources were. The boys were not slow to help Maria out and years later she proudly noted 'From the time of my daughter's marriage, my sons lived at their own cost'. Philip, aged 16, got a job doubling as clerk to a statesman and tutor to his sons, and Peter Paul, aged 13, became a page in the household of the Countess of Lalaing. There he must have gained some of the familiarity with court life that would stand him in such good stead later in his career. However, he did not stay long, for he had already decided that he wanted to be an artist, and his mother let him leave the Countess' service and become apprenticed to a painter called Tobias Verhaecht, who was a relative through marriage.

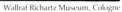

RUBENS' APPRENTICESHIP

Rubens spent only a short time with Verhaecht before moving to the studio of Adam van Noort. He spent about four years there and then went to study with Otto van Veen to complete his training. All three of these Antwerp painters were fairly mediocre and it is hard to know how much effect they had on Rubens, as very little of his early work survives (he was not a prodigy). Of the three, Van Veen must have been the man nearest to Rubens' heart. He had spent about five years working in Rome, and his thorough knowledge of Italian art was the basis for his successful career.

Rubens became a master in the Antwerp painters' guild in 1598, but he continued to work with Van Veen for another two years. Then, on 9

Mantua sojourn
(above) Rubens was 22 when he left Antwerp in 1600 for Italy and entered the service of Vincenzo Gonzaga, Duke of Mantua. The promising young artist still found time to paint himself with a group of friends he had made at the Ducal court.

The 'Costume Book'
(above right) These sketches of Turkish women come from an album of drawings Rubens compiled for visual reference. Of uncertain date, the collection may possibly range from before his Italian period to 1620.

Duke of Lerma
(right) By 1603 Rubens had sufficiently impressed the Duke of Mantua to be entrusted with a delicate political mission to Spain. During his rather uncomfortable stay he painted this splendid equestrian portrait of the Duke of Lerma, Philip III's supremely powerful first minister.

Prado, Madrid

13

Rubens in Rome

At the time when Rubens worked in the city, Rome was the artistic capital of Europe, not just because of the splendours of its remote – and recent – past but also because contemporary painters such as Caravaggio and Annibale Carracci had made it the centre of new developments, drawing artists from all over Europe. Rubens was particularly friendly with the German landscape painter Adam Elsheimer, whose poetic style influenced his own work in this field. But above all, Rubens took his inspiration from the great Renaissance masters of figure painting and the sculpture of the ancient world. So profound was his study of classical civilization that his friend Nicolas-Claude Fabri de Peiresc, a distinguished French antiquarian, later remarked that 'In the field of antiquity his knowledge was the broadest and most excellent I have ever encountered'.

Chiesa Nuova
(left) In 1606, during his second period in Rome, the rising young artist was offered an extremely prestigious commission over the heads of established resident painters – the high altarpiece for the Chiesa Nuova.

Copying the masters
(right) This exquisite sketch is Rubens' faithful copy of one of the Michaelangelo nudes on the Sistine ceiling.

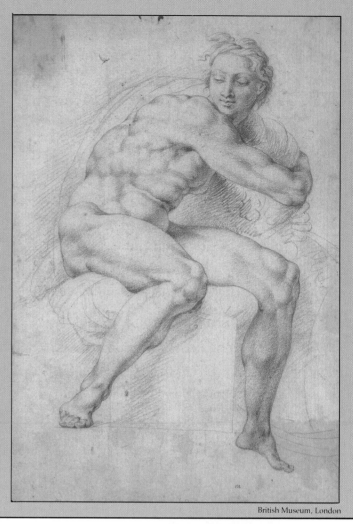

British Museum, London

May 1600, aged 22, he set out for Italy, accompanied by his first pupil, Deodatus del Monte. Italy was to be Rubens' base for the next eight years and to shape his artistic destiny. He went first to Venice where he was fortunate enough to meet an employee of Vincenzo I, Duke of Mantua, and impress him with his sketches. The Duke, too, was impressed when he saw them and immediately took Rubens into his service.

Vincenzo was a noted patron of the arts and working for him enabled Rubens to see many of the greatest treasures of Italian art. The art collection at the Ducal Palace in Mantua was superb, and part of Rubens' job was to make copies of famous paintings elsewhere to supplement it; within two years he had visited most of the foremost centres of Italian art, including Florence and Rome. His first visit to Rome lasted from summer 1601 to spring 1602, and it was at this time that he received his first public commission – three altarpieces for the church of Santa Croce in Gerusalame.

In 1603 Duke Vincenzo entrusted Rubens with a diplomatic mission, his first, taking gifts to Philip III of Spain. Two paintings were irreparably

Successful marriage
(right) On his return to Antwerp from Italy in 1609 Rubens met and married Isabella Brant. Their union, which was blessed with four children, was an extremely happy one, marked by mutual love and respect. After her death some 15 years later he professed that he had 'truly lost an excellent companion. She had no capricious moods, no feminine weaknesses, but was all goodness and honesty'. Praise indeed.

Uffizi, Florence

Antwerp palazzo
(right) In 1610 Rubens purchased a large house with extensive grounds in Antwerp. He added to and improved his property to such a measure that the original Flemish town house was transformed into a Renaissance palace complete with Baroque-style triumphal arch, formal garden, a pavilion and two studios. Though never to return to his beloved Italy, his mansion was to be a constant reminder of his stay there.

damaged by rain on the way and Rubens demonstrated his skill and presence of mind by promptly painting replacements. The Spanish royal family had an unrivalled collection of paintings by the great Venetian masters, above all Titian, so Rubens was able to continue his artistic education.

In 1604 Rubens was back in Mantua, but he did comparatively little original work for Vincenzo (who hardly made the best of his talents) and the most productive parts of the rest of his stay in Italy were once again spent in Rome; he was there, with gaps, from December 1605 to October 1608. In the second Roman period Rubens continued his diligent study of the art of the past and present while sharing a house with his brother Philip, who was now librarian to Cardinal Colonna.

Rubens by now had a growing reputation and good contacts and in 1606 he gained a prestigious commission to paint the high altarpiece for Santa Maria in Vallicella, a splendid new church (known in fact as the *Chiesa Nuova)*. This was one of the rare commissions with which he had difficulty. His first attempt was judged unsatisfactory, as the light reflected unpleasingly from it, so Rubens painted a replacement on slate, which was less reflective. He never saw the replacement installed, however, for in October 1608 he received news from Philip, now back in Antwerp, that their mother was seriously ill. Without delay, he travelled to be at his mother's side, but she died before he arrived.

RETURN TO ANTWERP

Before his mother's illness had caused Rubens to return home, the Archduke Albert, Regent of the Netherlands, had written to the Duke of Mantua requesting that the brilliant young painter should be released from his service, and now that circumstances had brought Rubens to Antwerp, Albert was not going to let him slip from his grasp. In 1609 Rubens was appointed court painter to Albert and his wife, the Infanta Isabella, and he was, in his own words, 'bound with golden fetters'. More tender links, also, were forged in that year, when he married the 17-year-old Isabella Brant, daughter of an eminent Antwerp lawyer and the niece of Philip Rubens' wife.

Rubens was soon besieged by pupils wanting to study with him, and in the next few years established and consolidated his reputation as the foremost painter in northern Europe. The works that most resoundingly proclaimed his genius were the two great altarpieces of the *Raising of the Cross* (1610-11) and *The Descent from the Cross* (1611-14) (pp. 24-5), which showed how completely he had mastered the Italian 'grand manner' – the way of treating lofty themes in the most heroic terms. His domestic life flourished, too. In 1610 he bought the land on which he erected a house of almost palatial splendour, and in the following year his daughter Clara Serena was born, the first of four

Albert and Isabella
(below) Rubens' decision to settle in Antwerp in 1608 came to the ears of the Archduke Albert and his wife Isabella, joint rulers of the Netherlands. The artist accepted the post of court painter with the proviso that he was not obliged to reside at the Brussels' court. When Albert died in 1621, Rubens became the Archduchess' trusted envoy to the fickle courts of France, England and Spain.

children by his wife Isabella.

This was an auspicious time for Rubens to launch into a new phase of his career, for there was a truce between the Northern (Protestant) and the Southern (Catholic) Netherlands (modern day Holland and Belgium) from 1609 to 1621, during which many churches were rebuilt or redecorated. Commissions flooded into Rubens' studio and he was able to execute them all only because of his incredible energy and formidable powers of organization, his assistants doing much of the actual physical act of painting, while the master provided the finishing touches. His constitution was very strong and he worked long hours, habitually rising at 4 am to go to Mass.

The greatest commission he received in Flanders was for the decoration of the Jesuit Church in Antwerp. This was a magnificent new building; Rubens had already supervized the sculptural decoration (he may well have had a hand in actually designing the building), when in 1620 he agreed to design 39 paintings which were executed by assistants (among them the young Van Dyck). The contract was signed on 29 March and the paintings were to be finished by the end of the year. Tragically, all the paintings were destroyed in a fire in 1718, but several superb sketches survive.

Great commissions came from abroad, too, and not just for religious works. Soon after the Jesuit

Joachim Blauel/Artothek

Royal Banqueting House Ceiling

The nine canvases that Rubens painted for the newly restored Banqueting House in Whitehall are the only works for major decorative schemes of his to remain *in situ*. Commissioned in 1629 during his diplomatic visit to England, they were finally despatched in 1635. So impressed was Charles I by the result that he presented the artist with a valuable gold chain and forbade the presentation of theatrical performances in the chamber for three years 'lest this might suffer by the smoke of many lights'.

Royal favour
(left) Charles I, greatly impressed by Rubens, knighted the artist-diplomat on the eve of the latter's return to Antwerp.

Artistic license
(right) The subject of the Whitehall canvases was the reign of the King's father James I. Rubens used his skills to raise his subject, who had been singularly unprepossessing both as man and ruler, to Olympian heights.

Scala

Detail: Van Dyck/Charles I of England and Henrietta of France

Bridgeman Art Library

Whitehall, London

and for her he travelled on missions to Spain in 1628-9 (where he charmed Philip IV and met his court painter, Velazquez) and to England in 1629-30, where he and the art-loving Charles I showed mutual warmth. Charles knighted him and also commissioned a series of paintings to decorate the ceiling of the Banqueting House, part of the Palace of Whitehall. Rubens painted these in Antwerp and they were sent to England in 1635.

In 1630 Rubens remarried. He was 53 and his bride, Hélène Fourment, the daughter of a prosperous silk merchant and the niece of Rubens' first wife, was 16. 'I resolved to marry again', he wrote, 'not yet being disposed to the austere celibate life . . .' Two sons still survived from his first marriage, and Hélène bore him two more sons and three daughters; he named one of them Isabella Hélène, after both wives. His love of his family shines through the paintings he made of them, and at this stage of his life he began to withdraw from public affairs to devote more time to them and to what he called his *dolcissima professione* or 'sweetest of professions'.

A BUSY RETIREMENT

In 1632 he asked Isabella to let him give up his diplomatic duties and in 1635 he bought a splendid country house, the Château de Steen, where he spent much of his time and indulged a new passion for landscape painting. He still worked hard in his studio in Antwerp, however, and the demand for his paintings was unceasing. In 1636 he embarked on one of his biggest commissions – 120 paintings of mythological subjects for the Torre de la Parada, a hunting lodge of Philip IV in Spain. Most of the finished work was done by assistants and Rubens was often unable to paint since his right arm was crippled with gout. The gout spread to his heart and he died in Antwerp on 30 May 1640, aged 62. Eight months later Hélène gave birth to their last child.

Winter love
(above) On his return from England, the 53-year-old painter became infatuated with and married Hélène Fourment, an Antwerp girl of 16 years. This painting is a self-portrait of the artist, his son and his pretty young wife.

Book illustrations
(above) From 1612 onwards Rubens regularly created title pages and occasional illustrations of complex and allegorical design for the Plantin press. This famous printing house was run by Balthasar Moretus, an early Antwerp friend.

Church contract
(below) In 1620 Rubens was commissioned to produce 39 ceiling paintings, two large canvases and various designs for a new Jesuit church in Antwerp. His studio rose admirably to the occasion, completing the work in nine months.

Church decorations were finished he designed a set of 12 tapestries showing the *History of the Emperor Constantine* for Louis XIII of France, and between 1622 and 1625 he carried out a series of 25 enormous paintings for Louis' mother, Marie de' Medici, to decorate her new palace (the Luxembourg) in Paris. This is one of Rubens' greatest achievements, in which he blends history, allegory and portraiture to create a glorious tribute to Marie's thoroughly inglorious life.

In 1626 Rubens' wife died. Although deeply distressed by the loss, Rubens was not a man to brood and he directed his energies not just into painting, but once again into diplomacy. His linguistic skills were put to good use in this role. Italian was as much his native tongue as Flemish, and he also had fluent French, German and Spanish, as well as Latin, which was still an international language. Particularly since the death of the Archduke Albert in 1621, he had become a trusted adviser to the Infanta Isabella,

The Effortless Genius

The artistic career of Rubens went from strength to strength, thanks to a reputation that was second to none: he was regarded as a fast, fluent worker whose confidence matched his versatility and ability.

Leda (c.1601-2)
(left) Rubens' sensuous rendering of the classical myth. Here Leda welcomes her lover, Jupiter, who is in the guise of a swan.

The Prodigal Son (c.1618)
(right) This favoured theme received the individual treatment of being set in a farmyard.

Rubens and Isabella Brant in a Honeysuckle Bower (1609-10)
(below) A tender portrait of Rubens and his first wife, Isabella.

Gemäldegalerie Alte Meister, Dresden

With the possible exception of Picasso, Rubens was the most prolific of all the great artists – so prolific, in fact, that it is difficult to put a figure on his huge output. He not only produced paintings on virtually every kind of subject, and the sketches and drawings for them, but he also designed tapestries, festival decorations, book illustrations and title pages and supplied visual directives for sculptors, architects and metalworkers. In 1621 he wrote 'My talents are such that I have never lacked courage to undertake any design, however vast in size or diversified in subject'. It sounds boastful, but it was simply a statement of fact, for he seemed to have limitless physical and intellectual stamina.

RUBENS' WORKSHOP

It hardly needs saying that Rubens was a fast and fluent worker – Sir Joshua Reynolds, who was an astute critic as well as a great painter, said that his works 'seem to flow with a freedom and prodigality, as if they cost him nothing'. Even Rubens, however, could not have handled the huge number of commissions he accepted without help, and his smoothly run workshop was essential to keep up the flow of work. We do not know how many pupils or assistants Rubens had at any one time, because his status as court painter exempted him from registering them with the guild. Certainly, he employed or collaborated with some of the outstanding Flemish artists of the day, notably Van Dyck and Jan Brueghel.

Joachim Blauel/Artothek

Alte Pinakothek, Munich

Musée des Beaux Arts, Antwerp

Arxiumas

Prado Madrid

Joachim Blauel/Artothek

Alte Pinakothek, Munich

Fall of the Damned (c.1620)

(left) Rubens painted this Baroque masterpiece – a scene of naked figures consigned to Hell – for the Jesuit church in Neuburg.

St George and the Dragon (c.1606-1610)

(above) From the colour, action and emotion of this painting we can see why Rubens was hailed as the 'Creator of Baroque'.

The degree to which Rubens worked on a painting himself depended on the significance of the commission and was reflected in the price. We are fortunate that a letter by Rubens survives listing some of his works for sale, in which he specifies some degrees of participation. He lists one painting, 'Original, by my own hand, the eagle painted by Snyders' (Frans Snyders, the greatest animal painter of the day); another, 'Original, by my own hand, with the exception of a most beautiful landscape, by the hand of a master skilled in the genre'; a third, 'begun by one of my pupils . . . but this, as it is not finished, would be entirely retouched by my own hand, and will pass as an original'; and a fourth, 'begun by one of my pupils. . . but all retouched by my hand'.

For a typical commission Rubens would paint a colour sketch (sometimes called a '*modello*'), his assistants would transfer this to a large-scale panel or canvas and Rubens would intervene at whatever stage he thought necessary. In the 20th century there has been a tendency to praise the sketches, in which the master's touch is visible in every stroke, at the expense of the finished work,

but Rubens would surely have found this attitude strange. It is often no easy task, even for experts, to determine where the assistant left off and Rubens took over, and the sketches, wonderful though they are, lack the scale and symphonic grandeur of the finished works.

Rubens' style was formed in Italy, on the example of the great painters of the Renaissance and the art of the ancient world, but there is much in his work that shows a continuance of Flemish tradition. The two great altarpieces that triumphantly set the seal on his reputation and his return to Antwerp – *The Raising of the Cross* and *The Descent from the Cross* (pp.24-5) – are in the form of triptychs with folding wings, a type long outmoded in Italy. And they are painted on panel, at this time more popular north of the Alps than in Italy. Rubens often painted on canvas, but he preferred panel, and he never used fresco, in Italy still regarded as the greatest test of a painter's mettle, but very rare in the damper north.

THE TRANSLUCENT TOUCH

The smooth panel on which he painted encouraged the fluency of Rubens' brushwork, which is so much a part of the feelings of movement and vivacity he excelled at conveying. He often used the paint very thinly, allowing the smooth white priming of the panel to shine through the layers of pigment and give an effect of glowing translucency. His brilliant painting of flesh has always been particularly admired. The Italian painter, Guido Reni, is said to have

Scala

Prado, Madrid

TRADEMARKS

Ample Flesh

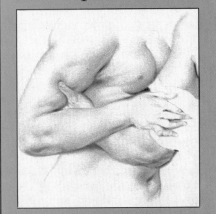

Rubens is probably best known for the voluptuousness of his female nudes. And these plump proportions appealed to him both as a man and as an artist: the curves of a well-fleshed woman were in fashion, and were also more interesting to paint.

The Three Graces (1639)
(above) Painted less than a year before Rubens died, these voluptuous hand-maidens reflect the artist's ideal of feminine beauty. Unlike his earlier, more vigorous and elaborate works, the serenity of this classically posed composition reveals a more mellow and reflective Rubens.

'Milk and blood'
(right) Rubens was renowned for his vibrant painting of flesh. His technique of using a special mixture of red, blue, yellow and white led people to describe the flesh of his ample female subjects as being made of milk and blood.

enquired, on seeing one of his pictures, whether he mixed his paint with blood.

Although so much of his career was spent as a public figure, and many of his most prestigious works were huge showpieces for church or state, his genius also had a much more private side, which found expression particularly in his tender portraits of his family and his loving depictions of the Flemish countryside. He rejoiced in the physical beauty of both his wives, and was obviously proud of his children's good looks, too. His landscapes and peasant scenes are now among his most popular works and show him to have been the heir to Pieter Bruegel, whose work he admired.

Rubens' work had enormous influence, both in his lifetime and in succeeding centuries. Hardly any significant Flemish painter of the 17th century was unaffected by his style, and his influence was spread to other countries not only by his voyages abroad and by the paintings exported from his workshop, but also by the engravings after his work that he commissioned. It is perhaps in France that he has had the most fruitful influence, Watteau, Delacroix and Renoir being three of the great French painters whose work is unthinkable without his example. In England, Constable was one his most fervent admirers and declared that 'In no branch of the art is Rubens greater than in landscape'. Rubens' genius, indeed, was so boundless that what to his contemporaries must have seemed like a sideline of his art could still, two centuries later, inspire one of the greatest of all specialists in the subject.

Portrait of a Little Boy (c.1619)
(below) Rubens was very much the family man and often used his children as models. The young subject of this affectionate sketch is thought to be his son Nicolas.

Albertina, Vienna

Bridgeman Art Library

Artists and their Wives

Artists have painted themselves and their families not only because they are convenient (and free) models, but also for any number of celebratory and commemorative reasons. Double portraits of the artist and his wife were perhaps most often painted to mark the couple's wedding, but the two examples here are rather different. Gabriel Metsu's charming portrayal of his wife and himself in an informal domestic setting embodies the peaceful well-being of Dutch bourgeoise life. The successful Adriaen van der Werff, however, belonged to a later generation – one which, quite obviously, had succumbed to the more mannered sophisticated influence of France.

Adriaen van der Werff (1659-1722) **Self-Portrait**
(right) Obviously proud of his wealth and status, Van der Werff uses the device of a picture within a picture to show off his porcelain-skinned wife and his splendid clothes and gold chain.

Rijksmuseum, Amsterdam

Gabriel Metsu (1629-67) **The Breakfast**
(left) Metsu belonged to the golden age of Dutch painting, a period when works, such as the one shown here, had an unpretentious vigour.

Rijksmuseum, Amsterdam

The Descent from the Cross

Rubens painted *The Descent from the Cross* in 1611-14 immediately after his other great altarpiece, *The Raising of the Cross*. Although they now hang together in Antwerp Cathedral they were not done as a pair. *The Raising* was painted for the church of St Walburga and was later transferred; *The Descent* was always intended for the cathedral. It was commissioned by the Guild of Arquebusiers, a military club, whose patron saint was St Christopher. The saint appears only on the outside of one of the wings, but throughout the whole work Rubens has honoured him by playing on the Greek meaning of his name – Christ-bearer. Thus, in the centre panel, Christ's limp body is borne down from the cross, and in the scenes at either side, *The Visitation* and *The Presentation in the Temple*, Christ is borne respectively in His mother's womb and by Simeon, the high priest of the Temple. Rubens' great altarpiece soon became famous and its influence was spread widely through engravings.

Making the modello
(left) For a large commission such as the one from the Arquebusiers, Rubens would have made preliminary sketches. This modello was painted in oil, before the contract was signed.

The Visitation
(below) In this detail the Virgin, heavily pregnant and dressed in travelling attire, arrives at Her cousins' house – portrayed by Rubens as a luxurious Renaissance villa.

Courtauld Institute, London

Mary Magdalene
(left) Mary Magdalene, portrayed by Rubens with his ideal of female beauty in mind, takes Christ's feet. Her flaxen hair hangs over one shoulder to remind us of the episode where she dried Christ's feet with her hair.

The elderly Simeon
(below) In this detail from the right-hand panel, The Presentation in the Temple, *we see the aged Simeon, clad as a high priest, holding up the Christ Child.*

'. . . this work has the power to touch a hardened soul.'

Roger de Piles (1677)

Antwerp Cathedral
(below) Begun in the 14th century and completed 200 years later, the Cathedral of the Holy Virgin in Antwerp remains the largest church and finest Gothic building in the city. As well as The Raising of the Cross *and* The Descent from the Cross *it also houses* The Assumption, *which is above the high altar.*

Classical pose
As is often the case with Rubens' subjects, the pose of the dead Christ has been borrowed from classical sculpture – in this case the main figure of the famous Laocoön *which is in the Vatican Museum, Rome.*

Gallery

Rubens' prodigious output was
for its range as well as its sheer
painted virtually every type of
was then known and his genius
that he excelled at everything h

His immense reputation was
primarily on his great showpiec
they were religious, such as Th

The Descent from the Cross *1611-14*
main panel 165″ × 126″, wings 165″ × 59″
Antwerp Cathedral

Rubens probably obtained the commission for this mighty work through his friend Nicholas Rockox, who was an official of the Guild of Arquebusiers, for which the altarpiece was painted. He included a portrait of Rockox in the right wing. The commission was given to Rubens in September 1611; he delivered the central panel in September 1612 and the wings followed in February and March 1614. Rubens drew freely on works he had seen in Italy for the composition and various details of the Descent, but he blended them into an inspired new whole. His superb colour sketches for the central panel and for the wings, representing The Visitation *(on the left) and* The Presentation in the Temple *(on the right) are in the Courtauld Institute Galleries in London.*

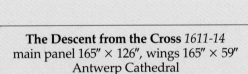

from the Cross, or secular, such as the Marie de' Medici cycle. Slightly more modest in scale, but still meant to be seen in grandiose settings, are works such as The Hippopotamus and Crocodile Hunt, one of the many works Rubens did for princely or aristocratic patrons.

The more private side to Rubens' genius comes out particularly in his portraits and his landscapes. He was at his best when painting people he was close to, as in Head of a Child and Le Chapeau de Paille (which probably represent his daughter and his sister-in-law). His landscapes are now among his most popular works, glorious evocations of the beauty and fecundity of nature.

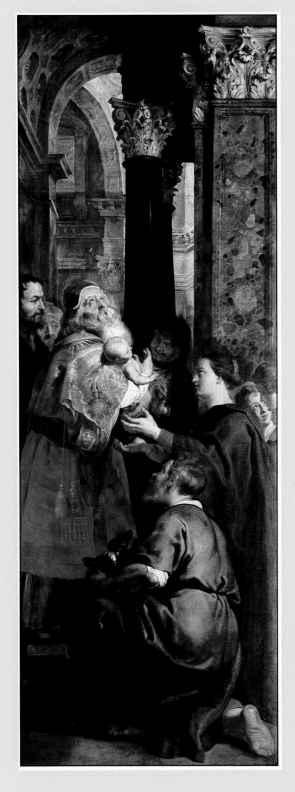

Hippopotamus and Crocodile Hunt *c.1615*
97¼″ × 126″ Alte Pinakothek, Munich

This is one of a series of four large hunting scenes that Rubens painted for Maximilian, Duke of Bavaria, for his palace at Schlessheim. He was assisted by Frans Snyders, who was acknowledged as the finest animal painter of the day. The various animals and humans are locked in a struggle that seems somewhat unlikely, but Rubens has composed and painted it with such overwhelming gusto that objections of this sort are soon forgotten. Rubens possibly derived the inspiration for the fight and furious grouping of men and animals from Leonardo's famous painting of The Battle of Anghiari, *of which he made a copy when he was in Italy. The fame of this hunting scene was spread by an engraving made after it by Pieter Soutman.*

Head of a Child *c.1618*
14½″ × 10½″ Vaduz Collection, Liechtenstein

The sitter has not been certainly identified, but it has been suggested that she is Clara Serena, the painter's eldest daughter, who died in 1623, aged 12. Such an intimate, informal portrayal would almost certainly be done for personal reasons. Rubens' father-in-law owned a portrait of Clara Serena, which may have been this one.

Le Chapeau de Paille *1620-25*
31″ × 21½″ National Gallery, London

It is something of a mystery how this famous painting got its traditional title, for the hat is clearly not of 'paille' ('straw'); the word may be a corruption of poil *(felt). The sitter was possibly Susanna Fourment, the sister of Rubens' second wife. It is probably Rubens' best-loved portrait, unsurpassed in the glowing painting of the flesh.*

The Education of Marie de' Medici *1622-25*
156″ × 117″ Louvre, Paris

*Rubens' great series on the life of Marie de' Medici is a triumph of
imagination over fact. Marie was a rather fat and unappealing figure,
but Rubens invests the trivial events of her life with Olympian
splendour. Here she is tutored by Minerva, the goddess of wisdom, and
other divinities, in a grotto on Mount Parnassus.*

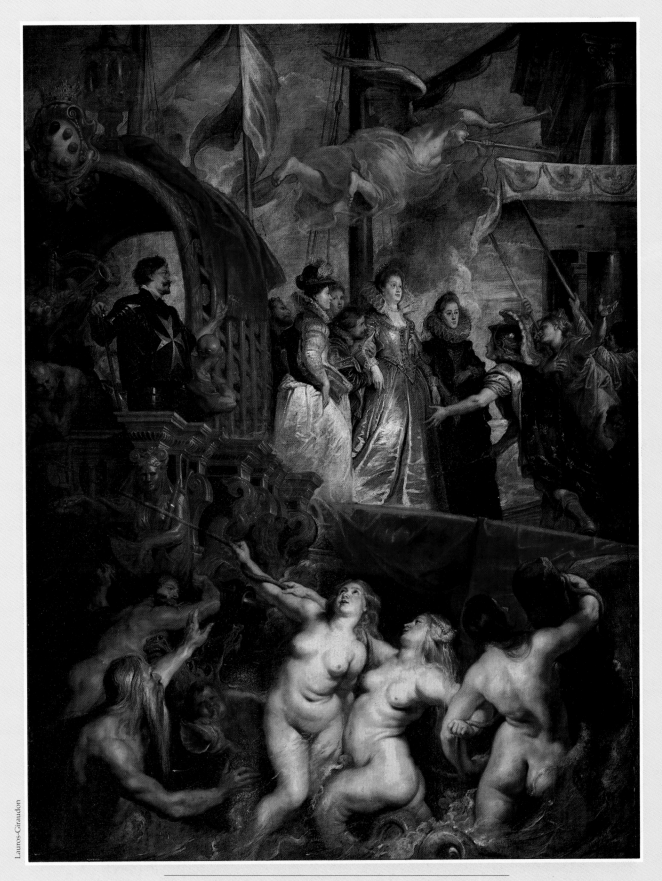

Marie de' Medici Arriving at Marseilles *1622-25*
156" × 117" Louvre, Paris

*In this, one of the most famous scenes of the Marie de' Medici cycle, the
future Queen of France arrives from Florence for her marriage to Henry
IV. She is greeted by an allegorical personification of France, while
above the figure of Fame sounds a clarion call on his trumpets. Sea-gods
and nymphs join in the celebrations.*

Autumn Landscape with a View of Het Steen c.1636
51¾" × 90½" National Gallery, London

Rubens bought the Château de Steen in 1635, and his son Albert told the French critic Roger de Piles that his father had done so in order to study landscape and paint in peace. This marvellously ripe and mellow painting is one of the greatest works that resulted from his decision.

Landscape with a Shepherd and his Flock c.1638
19½" × 33" National Gallery, London

Like the painting on the opposite page, this was a private work done for Rubens' own pleasure. The time of day in the Château de Steen picture is early morning, but here it is sunset and the mood is one of peace and tranquility. No wonder Rubens found painting such works therapeutic after the bustle of international politics.

The Feast of Venus
c.1630-40 85½″ × 138″
Kunsthistorisches
Museum, Vienna

*Few paintings convey,
more exultantly than this,
Rubens' love of life, in
particular life's sensuous
pleasures. The painting
centres on a statue of
Venus around which
celebrants are transported
by the delights of love.
Rubens' second wife,
Hélène Fourment, seems
to have been the model for
the girl on the extreme
left, and his pleasure in
her ample physical charms
no doubt played its part in
the inspiration of this
painting.*

Marie de' Medici

**One of Rubens' most ambitious decorative schemes was painted for
Marie de' Medici. It skilfully records the changing fortunes of the
Italian princess who became Queen of France.**

Bulloz

In the following September her first child – the Dauphin and future Louis XIII of France – was born at the Palace of Fontainebleau, near Paris.

In this way, Marie took her place at one of the most powerful courts in Europe. In 1600 the popular Bourbon King Henry IV governed 480,000 square kilometres and a population approaching 20 million. Designated 'the Great', Henry embodied the feudal qualities of kingship. Ruthless and autocratic, he demanded obedience: he led his troops into battle, excelled himself in hunting and sport and was famed for his sexual prowess – the court was littered with his mistresses and royal bastards.

COURT INTRIGUE

All power and privilege in France originated with the King, and court life was dominated by the manoeuvring and feuding of those who sought his favour. As Queen of France, Marie's position was relatively assured, but she suffered frequent humiliations through Henry's affairs and was often driven to fury by the presence of his favourite, Henrietta de Verneuil. Shortly after the birth of the Dauphin, Henrietta also produced a royal son, and she imperiously announced before Marie, Henry and the rest of the court that she had

Marie de' Medici was 26, and by all accounts a tall and handsome woman, when French ambassadors arrived at the Florentine court in 1599 to finalize arrangements for her marriage to Henry IV. This union between the Bourbons and the Medici was celebrated with all the pomp and circumstance due to such a momentous occasion. Marie's dowry included gold, costly jewels and the cancellation of all French debts to the Florentine republic. After a magnificent wedding ceremony – performed at the Duomo in Henry's absence – and a week of festivities, Marie set sail for Marseilles in a sumptuous galley bedecked with gold cloth, satin and precious stones, escorted by a flotilla of ships from Florence, Rome and Malta.

Marie first set eyes on Henry at Lyons, where their marriage was confirmed in November 1600.

A royal wedding
(above) The marriage of Marie de' Medici and Henry IV took place in Florence Cathedral on 5 October 1600. The Grand Duke of Tuscany stood in for Henry, who was too busy to leave France.

The King's mistresses
(right) Henry IV was notorious for his affairs. Gabrielle d'Estrées (on the right) bore the King three children.

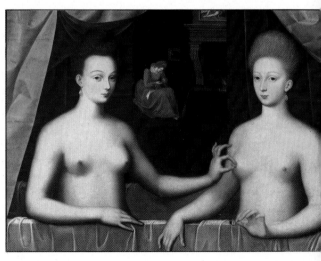

only given birth because the King had promised to marry her. Incensed, Marie drew back her arm to strike Henry and had to be restrained.

Outbursts such as this angered Henry, who frequently spoke of sending Marie and her entourage back to Italy. Henrietta vented her frustration and envy by publicly mimicking the Queen's gestures, voice and accent, while Marie was often heard to threaten the life of her rival.

Marie was no stranger to the licentiousness and intrigue which she found in Paris. Violent passions ran deep in the Medici family. Two of Marie's aunts were murdered by their husbands for infidelity. Her father, the Grand Duke Francesco I – founder of the famous Uffizi Art Gallery in Florence – was a notorious libertine, while his second wife, Bianca Capello, was rumoured to

have been a poisoner.

From this tempestuous yet cultured background, Marie brought a love of the arts, generosity and a blind devotion to her trusted followers. She was ambitious and vain, with an uncontrollable temper when provoked. Above all else she was committed to her Catholic faith.

In 1610, when the Dauphin was only nine years old, Henry was assassinated. Concerned to safeguard her own position and her son's inheritance, Marie established herself as Regent within hours of the King's death. For seven years she ruled France – as Queen Regent until 1614, when Louis reached 13 (the formal age of majority), and then for three years she was the president of his council.

Marie quickly surrounded herself with a

A popular monarch
(left) A shrewd politician, Henry strengthened the economy and built up a cohesive state after the religious wars, winning the trust of Protestants and Catholics alike.

The Queen Glorified
(above and right) Rubens recorded the major events in the life of Marie de' Medici in a magnificent series of 21 allegorical works painted for the Luxembourg Palace. In these two paintings Marie is depicted as Protector of the Arts (above) and as Regent of France (right). As Regent, she is taking over the reins of the state as Henry leaves to make war against Catholic Austria.

Marie's Italian advisers
(left) Leonora Galigai was Marie's friend and confidante for 17 years. In 1601 she married Carlo Concini, and together they exerted enormous influence over the Queen.

A gruesome fate
(below) On 24 April 1617 Concino – one of Marie's advisers – was murdered and Leonora taken prisoner. Concino was disinterred by the angry mob and mutilated.

dominant clique of Italians. She rejected many of the ministers who had advised Henry, mainly because they were Protestants, but took into her service clerics such as Richelieu whom she found useful and sympathetic. Her closest allies were Carlo Concino and his wife Leonora Galigai – a childhood friend from Florence. But Concini was predominantly preoccupied with self-aggrandisement and soon became dangerously unpopular at court because of his wealth and influence with the Queen Mother.

Despite her lack of sound advisers, Marie's period of government was free from major disasters. But it ended abruptly in 1617, when the young King turned against his mother and her friends. Acting on the advice of his trusted companion, Luynes, he sanctioned the murder of Concini. Marie's guard was disarmed, and the doors connecting her apartment with that of Louis were blocked. Marie and her remaining followers were exiled to Blois, but the unfortunate Leonora was charged with witchcraft and beheaded.

REBELLION AND RECONCILIATION

Marie's court in exile acted as a magnet for every discontented noble in France, and her supporters schemed to set her free. In 1619 she escaped and promptly joined forces with an uprising of grandees against the throne. After a decisive victory for the King at Ponts-de-Cé in 1620, Richelieu's mediation helped to bring about a reconciliation between mother and son.

Free to live in Paris once more, Marie returned to oversee the building of the Luxembourg Palace, modelled on her Florentine home, the Pitti Palace. In 1621 she invited Rubens to France and commissioned a series of paintings for the new palace. The Medici cycle was completed in 1625 and won a special visit from Louis XIII who expressed admiration for the great master's work.

But Marie's desire for political influence was by no means sated. In 1624, Richelieu, now a Cardinal, became Chief Minister to the King. Marie regarded him as her protégé and imagined that through him she might regain influence over Louis. But she was mistaken. Richelieu's loyalty was to the throne. Working carefully to keep

Exile to Blois
(right) Following the murder and imprisonment of her advisers in 1617, Marie de' Medici was exiled to the royal palace at Blois. There she regrouped her followers, including Richelieu, who became her chief adviser on 18 May. Only her children were denied her – a situation she tolerated much better than her loss of power. Feigning indifference, Marie schemed her return to Paris, finally escaping in 1619 to spearhead a new revolt against Louis.

Louis' trust and confidence, he pursued only those policies calculated to build Bourbon supremacy.

Early 17th-century Europe was dominated by the powerful and extensive Catholic Habsburg Empire of Austria and Spain. In 1618 a challenge to Habsburg rule from Frederick, the Protestant Elector Palatine of Bohemia, began the Thirty Years' War. Marie's instinct was to support the Catholic forces, but Richelieu held back from direct intervention. Concentrating on political rather than religious factors, he built alliances with the Protestant rulers of Germany and northern Europe. Eventually, in 1635, he declared war on the Habsburgs. By the middle of the century, when truces were concluded and fighting ceased, the French Bourbons under the Sun King, Louis XIV, were the greatest power in Europe.

Marie, however, had long since lost her influence over French policy. Throughout the 1620s she put pressure on Louis to adopt a foreign policy more sympathetic to the Habsburgs. When he fell ill in 1630, she insisted that it was divine punishment for neglecting his faith. During one terrible exchange it seemed that Marie had triumphed, and Richelieu prepared to flee Paris. But after reflection Louis reaffirmed his allegiance to the Cardinal. The outcome of this 'Day of Dupes' (12 November 1630) was the defeat of the Queen Mother and her faction, this time for ever.

Marie left France in 1631 and Richelieu made sure that she never returned and never again saw Louis. She sought refuge among the crowned heads of Europe and continued to intrigue against the Cardinal, hoping to regain favour at the French court, until her death in Cologne in July 1642. Marie's body was returned to France and interred beside Henry IV in the Basilica of Saint Denis.

Philippe de Champaigne/Sorbonne, Paris

Cardinal Richelieu
(above) Ambitious for power, Richelieu ingratiated himself with the King. In 1624 Louis made him Chief Minister, and for the next 18 years Richelieu worked tirelessly for the glory of France. He became Marie's most powerful opponent.

A life-like study
(right) Rubens made this drawing of Marie as a study for the Medici cycle. It is more realistic than the finished paintings which flattered Marie's ageing features. Known by the Parisians as 'the fat banker' in her lifetime, she died a poor, lonely figure in Cologne.

Victoria & Albert Museum

A Year in the Life 1630

1630 was a wonderful year for Rubens. The peace between England and Spain he had worked so hard for was finally concluded. A grateful King Charles I of England knighted him at their last audience and sent him away with the commission for a set of paintings that now ranks with his finest works – the ceiling of the Banqueting Hall in Whitehall. And in December, the artist married 16-year-old Hélène Fourment.

Rubens' graceful allegory *Blessings of Peace,* was painted for Charles to celebrate the new footing of Anglo-Spanish relations. It might also stand for the impression Charles wanted his new policy to create. Because war was so expensive, it threw the King at the mercy of Parliament to provide money. For Charles, Parliaments were nothing but trouble, using their control over taxation to blackmail the crown and meddle in

The Anglo-Spanish treaty of 1630, negotiated largely by Rubens, ushered in an era of peace – and tyranny – in England. Abroad, intrigue and conflict were rife and the fate of three great men – the German, Albert of Wallenstein, the Swede, Gustavus Adolphus and the Frenchman, Cardinal Richelieu – hung in the balance.

Seventeenth-century masterpiece
(below) One of Georges de la Tour's best known works, Magdalen with a Lamp *was painted around 1630. The artist's intense use of light and dark echoes that of Caravaggio.*

Louvre, Paris/Telarci-Giraudon

Giancarlo Costa

Boston founded
(right) When the puritan lawyer, John Winthrop, suddenly lost his lucrative appointment, he determined to leave England to start a new life in the Massachusetts Bay colonies with others of like faith. The immigrants reached Salem in June 1630 and after a brief stay in Charlestown founded the city of Boston on 17 September of the same year. Winthrop was to play a leading role in the history of the colony until his death in 1649.

politics. But with strict economy and avoidance of war the King could do without Parliament altogether. So in 1629 Charles adjourned Parliament indefinitely.

PROLOGUE TO CIVIL WAR

Some of his followers viewed Charles' period of personal rule as a golden age of peace and a time of happiness for the King. 1630 saw the reconciliation of Charles with his wife, Henrietta Maria, and the birth of their son, the future Charles II on May 29th. But for others it was 'the Eleven Years of Tyranny' and by 1630 opposition was beginning to mount.

One of the first victims of the tyranny was Sir John Eliot. In March of the previous year, Eliot had moved the Three

Resolutions in the House of Commons condemning the King's conduct – while his fellow members held down the Speaker to prevent him leaving the House and forcing an adjournment. In January 1630, Eliot was tried in the Court of King's Bench, fined £2,000 and detained at the King's pleasure in the Tower of London. Languishing in the Tower, Eliot contracted tuberculosis. Two years later, he was dead, giving the Parliamentarians a martyr and a hero.

Meanwhile, on the Continent, the great powers were still pursuing their age-old rivalries. France was still at loggerheads with the Habsburg Holy Roman Emperor and his Spanish relatives and the Spaniards were still trying to defeat the rebellious Dutch. For 12 years now, Germany had been ravaged by the Thirty Years' War (1618-48), as the struggle between

The tide turns
(left) Ferdinand II's hardline policy as Holy Roman Emperor on the enforcement of Catholicism throughout his realms began to collapse in 1630. This was due to the banishment of Wallenstein, the unwillingness of the electors to fall in with his plans and the arrival of Gustavus Adolphus of Sweden in Pomerania.

Connubial bliss
(right) This painting, completed c.1630, celebrates Charles I's newly discovered love for his wife Henrietta Maria, sister to Louis XIII of France. Testimony to the new marital harmony was the birth of their first child, the future Charles II during this year.

Daniel Mytens/Charles I & Henrietta departing for the chase

Giancarlo Costa

Swedish invasion
(left) Gustavus Adolphus landed with 4000 troops at Peenemünde, Pomerania, in early July 1630. The Swedish King was forced to enter the Thirty Years War after the Danish defeat at the hands of Tilly and Wallenstein. This had left the Baltic ports and their lucrative trade, controlled by Sweden, at the mercy of the latter general. Gustavus quickly raised support and by the following year was virtual master of Germany.

Protestants and Catholics, led by the Holy Roman Emperor, embroiled foreign powers.

For a few months in 1630, there was peace, with the Emperor Ferdinand apparently triumphant. But rifts had already appeared in the Catholic ranks. Ferdinand owed his supremacy to Albert of Wallenstein, Duke of Friedland, who had defeated the Danes and his other enemies. But the Emperor's allies did not trust Wallenstein, and Ferdinand himself suspected that this powerful soldier might have plans of his own. In August 1630, Ferdinand dismissed Wallenstein who retired gracefully to his estates in Friedland.

The action was badly mistimed, since a new Protestant champion had already appeared on the scene – and had already landed in Germany. In July 1630, the army of King Gustavus Adolphus of Sweden marched into Germany. Gustavus Adolphus' successes forced the recall of Wallenstein, but both men were doomed – Gustavus in the hour of his greatest victory at Lützen two years later and Wallenstein at the hands of assassins in 1634.

Wallenstein's downfall had been partly engineered by the wily French chief minister, Cardinal Richelieu – France had much to gain by the weakening of the Habsburg Empire. But Richelieu, too, had his enemies, including the Queen Mother Marie de' Medici. In November 1630, Marie believed she had persuaded Louis XIII to dismiss the Cardinal. But on the 12th, as Richelieu's enemies rejoiced, the King dropped a bombshell, confirming the Cardinal in his position indefinitely. The day was afterwards known as the 'Day of Dupes'.

Thwarted ambitions
(below) The year 1630 witnessed an eclipse in the dazzling career of Albert of Wallenstein. His entrepreneurial and managerial skills had created an army of 30,000 men spread throughout Germany, which was partially occupied in enforcing the Edict of Restitution. This entailed the restoration of Protestant property acquired since 1552. The presence of Wallenstein's army and his overweening ambition were unpopular with the Princes of both denominations. At their request, the Emperor dismissed his general.

Muchen, Neue Pinakothek

Catholic League
(left) The League was founded in 1609 by Maximilian, Elector of Bavaria, in opposition to the Protestant Evangelical Union under the Elector Palatine Frederick V. Committed to the Catholic cause, Maximilian was also aware of the political advantages to be reaped in the battlefield. His brother-in-law, the Emperor Ferdinand, wary of relying too completely on the army of the League under Count Tilly, had employed the services of Wallenstein. After the latter's dismissal in 1630 Tilly was once more sole Catholic commander.

Wallenstein retires to his country estates
(above) Though Protestant by birth, Wallenstein had profited hugely from the Emperor's ruthless policy towards Bohemians of that faith. By 1523 he owned about one quarter of Bohemia, centred in Friedland in the North. It was on these estates and in Prague that from 1630 he spent two years exile.

f Hals

c.1582-1666

One of the greatest portraitists of the 17th century, Frans Hals was born in Antwerp in the early 1580s. Shortly after his birth, his family moved north to Haarlem, where Hals was to stay for the rest of his life. Here he concentrated almost exclusively on painting local sitters. Unlike his great contemporary Van Dyck, Hals felt no inclination to travel, and was not concerned with the achievements of the great Italian masters.

Hals' remarkable style was formed largely in isolation and he was virtually self-taught. The strictly local character of his painting marked a new departure in Dutch art, and helped initiate the development of an independent Dutch school. Although he was successful, Hals lived most of his life in poverty, and the few known facts of his life reveal a series of domestic crises. He died in 1666, over 80 years of age.

The Convivial Portraitist

Hals lived and worked in Haarlem for his entire life. Although a highly successful portraitist, with the most prestigious sitters, he was plagued by financial troubles and died impoverished.

Frans Hals was born in Antwerp in 1582 or 1583, the son of Franchoys Hals, a cloth-worker from Mechelen, and Adriaentgen van Geertenrijck of Antwerp. It is not known when Hals' father moved to Antwerp, or when he married, but the couple seem not to have stayed long in the city, for by 1591 they had moved north to Haarlem, one of the largest towns in Holland. On 19 March 1591, Frans' brother Dirck was baptized in Haarlem. Dirck, too, became a painter, and is chiefly remembered for his lively genre scenes.

The family probably moved to Haarlem in, or shortly after, 1585, when Protestant Antwerp fell to invading Spanish forces. The Spanish re-established Catholicism in Antwerp, and the Protestants were given four years to settle their affairs and leave. In 1585, Franchoys had, in fact, declared himself a Catholic, but this could have been simply a tactical move. Like many of their contemporaries, the family may have moved north partly for religious reasons: the offical religion of the Northern Provinces was that of the Reformed Church, but other religions were treated with enlightened tolerance.

Franchoys' main reason for moving north was, however, probably a financial one. Following the Spanish victory, the Dutch effectively crippled trade with Antwerp by blocking the mouth of the River Scheldt. In the wake of the invasion, over 600 cloth-workers and their families migrated to Haarlem, which had a large textile industry, and the Hals family was almost certainly among them.

UNCERTAIN BEGINNINGS

Hals' own early years spent in Haarlem remain something of a mystery. An anonymous biographer of the Mannerist artist Karel van Mander included 'Frans Hals, portraitist' in a list of Van Mander's pupils. But Van Mander himself never claimed to have taught Hals, although he mentioned three of his other pupils in his *Schilderboeck* (The book of painters), published in 1604. It may be that Van Mander was reluctant to acknowledge an association with Hals. Certainly, the two men can have had little in common artistically, and Hals' lack of interest in history painting would not have impressed Van Mander. If Hals was one of his pupils, the relationship must have ended by 1604, when Van Mander is known to have moved to Amsterdam.

The first documented reference to Hals occurs in 1610, when he became a member of the Haarlem

L.Y. Loirat/Explorer

Key Dates

1582/3 born in Antwerp, Holland

c.1585 Hals' family moves to Haarlem, after the Spanish invasion of Antwerp

1591 birth of Dirck Hals

1610 enrols in the Haarlem Guild of St Luke

1616 paints the *Banquet of the Officers of the St George Civic Guard;* trip to Antwerp

1617 marries Lysbeth Reyniers

1622 paints *Couple in a Landscape*

1630/31 sued for debt

1662 granted aid by Haarlem town council

1666 dies in Haarlem

Hals' homeland
Frans Hals was born in Antwerp (above) although his family settled in Haarlem (right) shortly after. Haarlem lies on the River Spaarne in the westerly part of the Netherlands, an area dominated by large expanses of water. The town was a major centre of artistic activity, a position it had maintained since the 15th century. In Hals' time, Haarlem was enjoying great prosperity, one source of which was its breweries, whose beer had a great reputation.

'The Vasari of the North'
(left) Karel Van Mander founded an academy of painting in Haarlem where Hals may have studied. His 'book of painters' earned him the reputation as 'the Vasari of the North'.

First civic commission
(below) By 1616, Hals' reputation as a portraitist of renown was established and he received the first in a series of commissions from the Militia Companies for group portraits.

Banquet of the Officers of the St George Civic Guard Company/Frans Halsmuseum, Haarlem

Guild of St Luke. It was probably in the same year that he married for the first time. His wife, Annetje Harmansdr, bore him two children – the first, a son named Harmen, was baptized on 2 September 1611. The marriage did not last long, however, for Annetje died in 1615. She was buried in a pauper's grave – the first indication of the financial difficulties which were to plague Hals throughout the rest of his life.

MEMBER OF THE MILITIA

Hals' earliest known paintings also date from around 1610, by which time he must have been about 30 years of age. Even allowing for the loss of a number of earlier works, the few remaining facts suggest that Hals reached artistic maturity relatively late, and it was not until 1616 that he received his first major commission – for the group portrait of the *Banquet of the Officers of the St George Civic Guard Company* (this page).

Haarlem had two of these militia companies. Although their structure was military, their function was largely social, and they were renowned for their extensive banquets – in 1621 a law was passed stipulating that the banquets should last no more than 3 or 4 days. Unusually, Hals himself was a member of the St George Militia – membership was usually restricted to the ruling class, or to men of means – and he included his own likeness in his 1639 portrait of the officers of the Company. Hals' personal experience of the St

Militia headquarters
(below) Civic Guards proliferated in 17th-century Holland. Many had grand headquarters for which they commissioned large group portraits. With the demise of their military functions – when peace returned – these became mainly social clubs. By the late 17th century, the St George Civic Guard headquarters, illustrated here, had become an inn.

Hendrick C. Vroom/View of Haarlem from Noorder Spaarne/Frans Halsmuseum, Haarlem

HEEREN LOGEMENT

Dirck Hals/Merry Company in a Renaissance Hall/Akademie der bildenden Künste, Vienna

Hals' brother
Known chiefly for his lively interior genre scenes (above), Frans Hals' younger brother, Dirck, was also a painter of some repute.

Frans Hals Museum
(below) The Hals Museum in Haarlem, built in 1608, was formerly a home for old men. Today it has the best collection of Hals' work in the world.

Frans Halsmuseum, Haarlem

George Militia Company gave him a particular sympathy with their ideals, and enabled him to capture their conviviality and comradeship with unusual perceptiveness and skill.

In 1617 Hals married again. His second wife, Lysbeth Reyniers, was a peasant woman with a quarrelsome temper who is known to have been involved in brawls. She bore the artist at least eight children, three of whom went on to become painters. This ever-expanding family may account in part for Hals' continuing financial difficulties. Although he was undoubtedly successful as a portraitist, Hals was constantly in debt and in addition to his painting he undertook occasional picture-dealing and restoration work in order to make ends meet. In 1616 he was summoned to court for failing to pay maintenance to the guardian of the two children from his first marriage. Conveniently, the artist was away on a brief trip to Antwerp, and his mother answered the charge. During the 1630s Hals was sued by both his landlord and his shoemaker, and in 1654 a local baker seized his property because of an unpaid bill. The goods which Hals surrendered were pitifully meagre, amounting to three beds, pillows, some linen, an oak cupboard and table and five paintings, including one by Van Mander.

A STUBBORN WILL

There is, however, some evidence to suggest that Hals' difficulties were caused partly by his rebellious and independent spirit. In 1636, when he was in serious financial trouble, Hals refused to complete a lucrative commission for the portrait of an Amsterdam militia company which was known as *The Meagre Company*, because he was unwilling to make the relatively short journey out of Haarlem. When the guards refused to come to him, Hals downed tools, and the portrait had to be completed by another artist.

Judith Leyster

Judith Leyster was one of the most talented genre painters of the early 17th century, and the first recorded woman artist to be admitted to the Haarlem Guild of St Luke. It is not known if she was actually Hals' pupil, but she certainly came under his influence, and was the only contemporary painter who attempted to emulate his impressionistic technique. Leyster specialized in genre paintings, often depicting children, but she also painted still-lifes and portraits. Her husband, Jan Miensz Molenaer, was also a successful genre painter.

Gift of Mr and Mrs Robert Woods Bliss

National Gallery of Art, Washington

There was undoubtedly a strain of high-spiritedness in the Hals' family. In 1608, Frans' brother Joost was fined in Haarlem for insulting the city's guards, and for throwing rocks which injured a passer-by. Later, in the 1640s Frans Hals and his wife had their daughter Sara sent to a workhouse to improve her lax morals after she had given birth to an illegitimate daughter. Hals himself was apparently an enthusiastic drinker. According to the 17th-century biographer Arnold Houbraken, Hals was 'filled to the gills every evening,' although the popular image of the painter as an alcoholic and wife-beater is largely without foundation.

The 1630s were Hals' most successful years. By then he was in constant demand both for single portraits and for family groups, and was commissioned to paint three more large militia pieces. His sitters included men from the highest ranks of society – the city's regents, the civic guards, town councillors, merchants and scholars. Later, around 1649, he was to paint the famous

An austere interior
(above) Frans Hals was buried in St Bavo's Church in Haarlem in 1666. This view of the church interior by the architectural painter, Pieter Jansz Saenredam, conveys the bareness of the churches at that time. This was due to the Protestant order that walls be whitewashed and all visual imagery banned.

French scholar René Descartes. Hals was also running a successful studio, although he does not seem to have used his pupils as assistants, and few of them were able to imitate his unique style. Nonetheless, the list of his students includes some of the most distinguished names in Dutch painting, such as his own brother Dirck, and the brilliant genre painter Adriaen Brouwer. The talented Judith Leyster also came under the influence of Hals, and she may even have been a pupil. However, the two artists obviously quarrelled and in 1635 she sued Hals for accepting an apprentice who had defected from her studio.

FINANCIAL HARDSHIP

Hals' success continued until the end of his life, although he suffered a slight drop in commissions after 1640, which may reflect the growing enthusiasm in the Netherlands for the more elegant style of Van Dyck. Nevertheless, it was during his last years that Hals produced some of his best portraits, such as *The Regentesses* (p.49) with its haunting vision of old age.

Hals' financial troubles, however, continued. In 1661 the Guild of St Luke exempted him from payment of his dues, and in 1662 he petitioned the town-councillors for assistance. The following year he was granted an annual subsidy of 200 guilders, and in 1664 they provided him with three cartloads of peat. Hals died two years later, on 29 August 1666, over 80 years of age. He was buried in St Bavo's Church in Haarlem.

Self-Portrait
(left) The self-confident look in Leyster's lively portrait is that of a female painter in a man's world.

A Boy Playing a Flute
(above) This charming painting is typical of Judith Leyster's work: full of life and realistic detail.

Painterly Bravura

Hals' portraits have a spontaneity and vitality that bring his sitters to life, giving us a vivid impression of the personalities of the men and women who created the thriving Dutch Republic.

Hals was not only the first great master of the Golden Age of Dutch painting, but also one of the most original and distinctive portraitists of any school or period. Almost all his 300 or so surviving paintings are portraits, and even those that are not (some genre scenes and a very occasional religious piece) have a portrait-like character. He was obviously fascinated with faces, and his work brilliantly captures the personalities of the men and women of the buoyant generations that – after winning freedom from Spanish domination – turned Holland into the most prosperous country in Europe.

The qualities that make Hals' portraits so exceptional were well characterized by his contemporary, Theodorus Schrevelius, a Haarlem schoolmaster who in 1648 published a history of the city called *Harlemias*. In an enthusiastic passage on Hals, he wrote: 'By his extraordinary manner of painting, which is uniquely his, he virtually

Laughing Boy 1620-25
(right) The artist painted several genre scenes of children, usually showing them in simple and endearing activities such as playing musical instruments or blowing soap bubbles. Most of them can be interpreted as representations of one of the five senses or as variations on the vanitas *theme, but this laughing boy seems to carry no such meaning. Hals simply painted him as a study in fleeting expression, capturing his laughter in a few swift brushstrokes.*

Mauritshuis, The Hague

Rijksmuseum, Amsterdam

The Merry Drinker 1628-30
(left) Portraits of drinkers were commonplace in Dutch art. Many of the pictures had a moralizing intention, but Hals' subject has a sparkle and vigour that advertises the pleasures of drink only.

Portrait of a Seated Woman c.1660
(right) Hals was a master of different moods. The quiet dignity of this unknown woman presents an interesting contrast to the swaggering stances seen in some of the male portraits.

surpasses everyone. His paintings are imbued with such force and vitality that he seems to defy nature herself with his brush.'

Schrevelius, who sat to Hals for his portrait, neatly identified the two outstanding features of Hals' work – his unique brushwork, or 'manner of painting', and the 'force and vitality' of his characterization.

ENERGETIC BRUSHWORK

For Hals, these two qualities were inseparable. The 'force and vitality' of his portraits depends directly on his brisk, energetic brushwork, which gives to his sitters an irresistible appearance of life. Netherlandish portraits before the time of Hals were painted with a high degree of finish, the brushstrokes carefully blended to create a smooth, polished appearance. By contrast, Hals' brushwork seems daringly free; his brushstrokes are brusque, swift and disconnected, particularly

Willem van Heythuyzen 1637-39
(above) Hals portrayed his subject in a very daring attitude, tipped backwards on his chair so that his body forms a strong diagonal across the picture plane. The artist usually employed plain backgrounds, but here he found it necessary to balance the sitter's precarious pose by including the room behind him.

The Regentesses 1666
(below) Hals transformed the apparently unpromising subject of four elderly governesses and their servant into a fascinating portrayal of old age. He did this by emphasizing the individual character of each face and by giving particular prominence to the gnarled hands, which are arranged to form a rhythmic pattern against the shadowy background.

in his more informal portraits such as the enchanting *Laughing Boy* (opposite). Here, the boy's face is modelled in rough strokes of colour, so free that we can distinguish each separate mark of the brush, especially in the painting of the eyes. The spontaneous 'improvized' appearance of the work is increased by the fact that, unlike previous painters, Hals did not stop to blend the tones and colours used in the face, but placed strokes of contrasting colour directly side by side.

Although at first glance Hals' technique might appear arbitrary, he placed his brushstrokes with unerring precision. His paintings are not abstract combinations of tones and colours – his brushstrokes model the shapes and forms of his sitters with remarkable exactness, and are the result of painstaking observation. In *Malle Babbe* (p.63), for example, Hals' apparently carefree brushstrokes capture to perfection the dance of light across the surface of an aged face that is momentarily crumpled with laughter. In *The*

Regentesses (p.49), rough dabs of paint model the knotted, tremulous hand that is lying stiffly in the lap of an elderly woman.

SPONTANEOUS METHODS

Hals achieved these effects by adopting a fairly simple working procedure. No drawings by him are known, and he seems to have worked directly onto the canvas without preliminaries. The light in his portraits always comes from the left, from a single source, and by working in this way, he developed a deep and instinctive grasp of the appearance of different types of face under a specific light source. Having mastered this basic problem, Hals could study the individual variations produced by each sitter in minute detail, reproducing them with a few confident strokes of the brush. This spirited brushwork bestowed on his sitters a unique vitality and life. We see his sitters not as fixed or permanent images, but as individuals caught in a passing moment, with a fleeting, transitory expression.

The composition of Hals' portraits is also relatively simple. Unlike Van Dyck, for example, who created a complete environment for his sitters, Hals placed his sitters against a plain background, focusing attention primarily on the face which was for him the main object of interest. For similar reasons, perhaps, Hals' portraits are mainly head-and-shoulders or half-length portrayals; with the exception of group portraits he painted only one full-length.

The liveliness of Hals' approach is seen also in the way he modified the poses of conventional portraiture to make them more informal. One of his favourite devices was to place the sitter seated, with his arm over the back of the chair, turning round to face the spectator as if we had suddenly caught his attention. The turning pose was not exactly new – it had been a standard feature of portraiture since the Renaissance. Hals, however, gave the motif a greater immediacy, by sharpening the twist of the body.

Another of Hals' favourite compositional schemes was to show the sitter with arms akimbo, an elbow projecting towards us out of the picture space. Hals used this device to particularly good effect in his early militia pieces, such as *The Banquet of the Company of St George* where several of the men turn towards us with their hands on their hips, as if suddenly disturbed at their revels.

TECHNICAL VARIATIONS

Hals did sometimes modify his style to suit the demands of a particular sitter, or commission. In the *Laughing Cavalier*, for example, the confident and self-assured sitter was clearly anxious to display the sumptuous embroidery on his sleeve (p.57 and opposite). This exquisite decoration offers a clear demonstration both of the sitter's wealth and of his personal taste. Accordingly, Hals has painted the embroidery with small, neat strokes which capture

Symbols and Emblems

During the 1620s and 30s Hals painted a number of lively genre scenes. Like most genre paintings, these make abundant use of symbols and emblems. Such devices were enormously popular in Dutch art, and added a rich complexity of meaning to scenes which, to the modern eye, might appear quite straightforward. While some of Hals' symbols are self-explanatory, others are more obscure and derive from contemporary emblem literature. Emblem books, which originated in the 16th century, contained collections of pictures or pictorial devices, which were given a symbolic meaning by a motto or inscription. These books enjoyed a tremendous vogue in Hals' time, and artists often used them as a source of symbols, confident that the viewer would be able to recognise and to understand fully their true significance.

Bequest of Benjamin Altman, 1913

The Metropolitan Museum of Art

The Shrovetide Revellers
(above) Two of the figures represent characters from theatre; the Hans Wurst, with the sausage hanging from his cap, and Pickle Herring, with the herrings in his festival garland. A *herring was the symbol of a fool, as was the fox-tail held by Pickle Herring. The spoon in the third man's hat is a symbol of greed, while the sausages and the bag-pipes have erotic associations.*

National Gallery, London

A Young Man Holding a Skull

(above) This has often been thought to represent Shakespeare's Hamlet soliloquizing on the death of Yorick. In fact it is probably a vanitas *image, designed to remind the viewer of the transience of earthly life. The skull was a common symbol of death and was often included in portraits, to remind the sitter of his own mortality. Here, the boy's vitality and youthful charm lend a particular poignancy to this solemn reminder of death.*

Emblematic Embroidery

(left) This complex image of Mercury's cap and staff comes from the Emblematum Libellus *of Andrea Alciati, a popular emblem book which was published in 1534. A similar device appears on the sleeve of the* Laughing Cavalier *and no doubt had a personal significance for the mysterious sitter. Other emblematic devices on the cavalier's sleeve (below) include flaming cornucopias, winged arrows, lovers' knots and bees. These were all familiar elements in emblems on love. These fascinating details, lovingly depicted by Hals, are displayed by the sitter with ostentatious care.*

The Wallace Collection

The Prodigal Son in a Tavern

(left) This may seem like a simple scene of a drinker and his sweetheart, but it almost certainly depicts the Prodigal Son carousing in a tavern, a common theme in Dutch art, and one with clear moral overtones. The dog symbolizes greed and unchastity.

The Metropolitan Museum of Art

Informal Poses

A characteristic feature of Hals' portraits is his use of informal poses, especially for his male sitters. Often, his subjects lounge casually in a chair, or stand turned towards us, as if suddenly disturbed. These devices give Hals' portraits an unequalled spontaneity and liveliness.

Bildarchiv Preussischer Kulturbesitz

Staatliche Museen, Berlin

the intricate details and suggest the richness of the stitching. By contrast, the plain cuff and the sash around his waist are painted in a relatively free manner. In the *Portrait of Isabella Coymans* (p.67), Hals varies his brushwork to similar brilliant effect. Her face is painted with carefully blended brushstrokes to suggest her smooth, healthy complexion, while her jewellery and clothing are painted with the roughest dashes of colour.

THE BEAUTY OF BLACK

In the *Family Group* (p.65), Hals' technique is altogether more restrained. During the 1640s fashion in the Netherlands had in fact become more subdued, with sober black costumes becoming *de rigeur* for the well-to-do. Hals has painted the respectable family, particularly the older members, with due respect for their sobriety and discretion. At the same time, the painting demonstrates how Hals could create interest even within a simple expanse of black cloth, by subtly varying his tones. It may have been a painting such as this which led Van Gogh to exclaim that 'Frans Hals has not less than 27 blacks'.

Hals' greatest gift, however, was his talent for characterization. Each one of his sitters is a distinct individual captured, we feel, with their most characteristic expression. Hals' unique genius in this respect is seen most clearly in his large militia

pieces. Commissions such as this presented a particular problem for the artist, who was faced with the task of arranging a large group of figures in such a way that each face was equally visible, and no individual given undue prominence. At the same time, he had to avoid the monotony of placing each figure facing towards the front, as if the painting was a school photograph. Hals solved these problems superbly. In the *Banquet of the Officers of St George*, for example (p.45), he creates an impressive variety by placing the heads of the figures at continually contrasting angles. But the real variety is in creating an array of perfectly characterized individuals. Around the crowded table we see a gallery of personalities and expressions from the cautious, enquiring elderly man, to the confident young ensign, and the delightfully jovial and humorous Colonel seated at the table's head.

Hals was one of the first generation of Dutch painters to live and work exclusively in Holland and this had important implications for his art. Whereas the previous generation of Dutch artists had looked to Italy for their inspiration, Hals had little interest in Italian art with its emphasis on historical subject-matter and its concept of ideal human beauty. He took his subjects from everyday life and portrayed the Dutch people he saw around him. Hals does not appear to have flattered or idealized his sitters. As far as we can

Boy with a Flute
1623-25
(above) This is one of a series of paintings – including Young Man Holding a Skull *(p.51) – that show the type of single genre figure that was popular in Dutch art from the 1620s onwards. Hals used the genre in a particularly original manner, deploying strong directional lighting and bold diagonals, and eliminating detail in favour of the overall dramatic effect. The raised hand (right) – suggested by a few slashes of paint – shows that the boy has been interrupted mid-gesture, adding to the animation of the scene.*

tell, he did not modify or 'improve' their features to conform to an accepted standard of beauty. He seems to have shown them exactly as they were with all their peculiarities, and the individuality of their features. It is this which enables us to identify with Hals' sitters as flesh-and-blood personalities. Van Gogh paid a moving tribute to this feature of Hals' painting when he wrote to his brother Theo from Antwerp: 'My thoughts are all the time full of Rembrandt and Hals, not because I see so many of their pictures, but I see among the people here so many types that remind me of that time.'

A LASTING REPUTATION

Van Gogh wrote at a time – the 1880s – when Hals' reputation was at its height. After being almost forgotten for many years after his death, he became a major influence on *avant-garde* French painters such as Manet, who admired the spontaneity of his brushwork. Society portraits were taken with his verve and panache, and he became a particular favourite with American collectors, which explains why so many outstanding works by him are in the USA. From about 1870 to about 1920 Hals was without doubt one of the most popular of the Old Masters. Since then, his status has slipped a little, perhaps because of the almost inevitable comparisons with Rembrandt – a comparison that only a handful of the world's greatest artists could sustain. To be Holland's second greatest portraitist, is, however, no mean distinction.

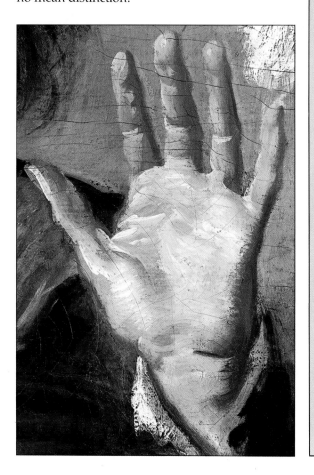

Single-figure Genre Painting

The tradition of single-figure genre painting originated largely in the work of the 17th-century Italian painter Caravaggio. Drawing on the works of earlier Flemish artists Caravaggio painted numerous single figures in exotic dress. His achievements were introduced into the Netherlands by the Utrecht Caravaggisti, a group of Dutch artists such as Gerrit van Honthorst, who had been to Rome and seen his works at first hand. Hals was also greatly influenced by the various figures of the Caravaggisti.

Gerrit van Honthorst (1590-1656) **The Merry Fiddler** *(left) Single genre figures often represent one of the Five Senses. The exact significance of this figure is unclear – it has been suggested that he personifies either Taste or Hearing. But where the artist intended an allegorical meaning this is usually made clear, and the inclusion of both a violin and a wine-glass makes the figure rather ambiguous.*

Rijksmuseum, Amsterdam

Edouard Manet (1832-83) **The Spanish Guitarrist** *(right) Manet said of his exotic guitar-player: 'In painting this figure I had in mind the Madrid masters, and also Hals'. Single genre figures were also popular in 17th-century Spain, and among the 'Madrid masters' Manet was probably thinking primarily of Velásquez – he was certainly influenced by Velásquez's painting technique. Musicians also figure largely in Hals' work.*

Gift of William Church Osborn, 1949

The Metropolitan Museum of Art

Married Couple in a Garden

The subjects of this delightful portrait can probably be identified as the merchant and explorer, Isaac Massa, and his first wife, Beatrix van der Laen. Massa had his own portrait painted twice by Hals and the features in these works correspond closely with those of the sitter here. The portrait was probably painted to commemorate the couple's marriage, on 25 April 1622. It is certainly a marriage portrait for the woman clearly displays her ring, worn here on the index finger, in line with contemporary fashion.

The portrait illustrates particularly well Hals' genius for creating informal images; the couple appear to have just moved away from the company on the lawn, to enjoy a moment alone in a secluded bower. The woman's shy smile and affectionate gesture add to the informality of this charming work so gracefully displaying Hals' expertise.

Contrasting textures
(above) Hals captures perfectly the contrast between the dull texture of the fine lace collar and the black of Massa's coat.

A merry company
(right) These elegant couples in the park recall outdoor merry company scenes, and reinforce the mood of happiness.

Rijksmuseum, Amsterdam

Bequest of Frank P. Wood, 1955

Art Gallery of Ontario, Toronto

Isaac Massa
(left) Hals painted this fine portrait of Massa in 1626, about four years after the wedding picture. According to the inscription on the chair Massa was then 41. He was a merchant, explorer and cartographer, who had commercial interests in Russia. It has been suggested that the view of a landscape, which is unusual in Hals' portraits, refers to his activities in foreign parts.

Symbols of love
(right) The portrait contains several symbolic objects. The ivy symbolizes steadfast love, and the vine stands for marital love and dependence. Peacocks are sacred to Juno, goddess of marriage, and the wedding ring symbolizes marital union. The broken urn may signify the passage of time.

An emblem of fidelity
(above) There was a well-established tradition of depicting pairs of lovers in a garden setting. In this woodcut from Alciati's emblem-book, the lovers with clasped hands symbolize conjugal fidelity.

Sally Holmes

Gallery

Hals was almost exclusively a portraitist and he was equally a master with paintings of men, women and children, double portraits and group portraits. The sitters in Hals' paintings usually seem to enjoy life, and no other painter has depicted smiles and laughter so convincingly, as is shown so memorably in such varied works as The

Nurse and Child *c.1620*
33¾" × 25½" Staatliche Museen,
West Berlin

This is one of the most captivating of Hals' early works. The woman and child are observed with great freshness and look out as if they had just been diverted by the spectator. Although he is renowned for the boldness of his brushwork, Hals showed here how beautifully and delicately he could paint elaborately detailed costume when the occasion demanded. The sex of the child is uncertain, as boys and girls this young were dressed alike at this period so it was difficult to tell them apart.

Bildarchiv Preussischer Kulturbesitz

Laughing Cavalier, The Gipsy Girl, Malle Babbe and Isabella Coymans.

It is perhaps in his group portraits that Hals best shows his remarkable skill in characterization (as well as his inventiveness in composition). His two pictures of A Family Group in a Landscape and his Married Couple in a Garden convey the ordered contentment of a society that in its modest way marks one of the high points of European civilization. And The Banquet of the Officers of the St Hadrian Civic Guard Company, one of a remarkable series of such pictures, is a triumphant portrayal of warm and high-spirited comradeship and a tour de force of technical virtuosity.

The Laughing Cavalier *1624*
33¾″ × 27¼″ Wallace Collection, London

Apart from the Mona Lisa, this is probably the most famous portrait in the world. Its great fame came fairly late, however, and its familiar but inaccurate title (the sitter is smiling rather than laughing) did not appear in print until 1888. In the 18th century it fetched fairly modest prices at auction, but in 1865 Lord Hertford bought it for 51,000 francs, a sensational sum that heralded the great boom in Hals' popularity.

57

Married Couple in a Garden *c.1622*
55″ × 65½″ Rijksmuseum, Amsterdam

Various factors indicate clearly that this is a marriage portrait: the woman displays her wedding ring (it had become fashionable to wear it on the index finger rather than the third finger); the ivy on the ground is a traditional symbol of love and faithfulness; and lovers were often portrayed in a garden, one of the abodes of Venus. Hals' painting is reminiscent of Rubens' famous double portrait of himself and his first wife, which he could have seen when he visited Antwerp in 1616, but Hals has made the composition boldly asymmetrical by placing the couple to one side. There has been much speculation about the identity of the sitters, although the once popular idea that they represent Hals and his second wife has now been discounted. The size and splendour of the painting, however, suggest that the young couple were people of means, and it is now thought that they are the wealthy merchant Isaac Massa and his wife Beatrix van der Laen.

**Banquet of the Officers of
the St Hadrian Civic Guard
Company** *c.1627*
72″ × 105″ Frans Hals
Museum, Haarlem

*This group portrait was
probably painted in 1627 to
mark the farewell banquet given
to the officers of the company
after they had served their term
of office. As with all his civic
guard portraits, Hals succeeds
brilliantly in conveying the
animation of a crowd of figures,
each officer individualized but
integrated into an organized
composition.*

Gipsy Girl *c.1628-30*
22¾″ × 20½″ Louvre, Paris

This has long been one of Hals' most popular works. The handling of the paint is brilliantly free and spontaneous and the overall effect one of extreme vivaciousness. The girl's smile has been described as 'a sort of low-life answer to the Mona Lisa'; her low-cut costume indicates that she is a prostitute.

Malle Babbe *c.1630-33*
29½″ × 25¼″ Staatliche Museen, West Berlin

*Nothing is known of Malle Babbe (the name is recorded on the wooden
stretcher of the canvas), but she must have been a formidable character.
The owl on her shoulder is a curious detail; it is now usually associated
with wisdom, but in the past it symbolized many qualities, including
drunkenness.*

Family Group in a Landscape c.1648
79½" × 112¼" Thyssen-Bornemisza Collection, Lugano

The identity of the family is unknown, but the black servant may indicate that the man had connections with the West Indies. It is thought that the background is by Pieter de Molyn, a Haarlem landscape specialist.

Family Group in a Landscape c.1648
58½″ × 98¾″ National Gallery, London

The picture has been cut at the top, so its proportions would once have been more similar to the painting above. Here, too, the landscape background is probably by Pieter de Molyn.

Stephanus Geraerdts *c.1650-52*
45½″ × 34½″ Musée Royal des Beaux-Arts, Antwerp

*Stephanus Geraerdts was an alderman and councillor of Haarlem. This
and the portrait of his wife (opposite) form a pair linked by action
between the two figures, a fact that makes it lamentable that the
paintings have been separated. The sitters are identified by their coats
of arms in the background of each picture.*

Isabella Coymans *c.1650-52*
45¾″ × 33¾″ Private Collection

Hals rarely painted a more beguiling figure than this or a more charming smile. Isabella turns to hand her husband a rose, and there is a telling contrast between his corpulent seated figure and her slender young body. The details of the costume are painted with panache and the painting radiates a sense of warmth and life.

IN THE BACKGROUND

Dutch Independence

The bitter struggle between the Netherlandish provinces and their Spanish overlords lasted for almost a century, and ended in the creation of the modern Dutch nation.

In 1585, Alexander Farnese, Duke of Parma, seized Antwerp for the Spanish, and the Hals family amongst others moved north to Holland. Since the real start of the Netherlands revolt in the 1560s, thousands of refugees had left the southern provinces, taking their skills and wealth to the independent North or even abroad. Seventeen northern Netherland provinces were uneasily united in a Calvinist-organised rebellion against the Spanish overlords; the revolt was sustained by profits from Dutch trade, and given some respectability by the leading noble family, The House of Orange.

Spanish foreign interests were too widespread, and resources were never concentrated to crush the Netherlands. When Phillip II of Spain died in 1598, he left his daughter Isabella and her husband Albert to rule the southern Netherlands, with orders to curb the success of the so-called United Provinces. In effect, the Low Countries were partitioned into a Protestant North and a Catholic South – which roughly corresponded to the modern nations of Holland and Belgium.

Isabella and Albert, known as the Archdukes, had a personal sympathy with the land they governed. In 1609, a 12 year truce was signed between the equally exhausted Spanish and Dutch, and the Archdukes set about repairing the devastated South. They achieved an economic and spiritual regeneration: the population rose, trade and industry recovered and Catholicism launched a missionary offensive against Protestantism. This enlightened government gave the southern Netherlands a sense of itself: an embryonic national identity, which enabled it to survive the later Dutch and French invasions when Spanish aid was limited.

War had helped unify the United Provinces,

Fishing for souls
(below) The Dutch artist Adriaen van der Venne used Christ's promise 'I will make you fishers of men' to make an ironic comment on the jealousy that existed between the rival religious powers of the Dutch Republic and Spain. The Dutch Protestants on the left bank face the Spanish Catholics on the right, while in the centre boats from both sides compete with each other for the capture of the souls of the innocent.

Rijksmuseum, Amsterdam

The Spanish fury
(left) The Spanish ruled the southern Netherlands by terror. A horrifying incident of their brutality occurred in 1576, when the Spanish garrison in Antwerp mutinied and sacked the city, pillaging property and killing without mercy. When the city fell to the Spanish in 1585 many Flemish Protestants fled to the North, fearing for their lives.

and the ceasefire of 1609 showed up the differing factions. The House of Orange needed military command to maintain its power, while the province of Holland (the richest and therefore the strongest in the union) desired peace. War had been expensive, and since 1605 the Spanish Army had been led by the able Spinola and little had been achieved by the United Provinces. In addition, the Spanish were heaping up embargoes on Dutch trade – a particularly effective form of warfare. But the 12 year truce was not an idle time for the Dutch. An unofficial war continued in the form of pirating trade in the Spanish colonies, while the government of the United Provinces concluded alliances with Spain's enemies. The idea was to divert Spanish resources away from the Netherlands to other trouble spots. So the Dutch formed a series of Islamic alliances – with Morocco in 1608, the Ottoman Empire in 1611 and Algiers in 1612, and soon became the chief supplier of arms to North Africa.

AN INDEPENDENT NATION

The Truce of 1609 had at least one effect the Spanish had cause to regret: the acceptance of the Dutch as an independent nation by other world powers. Consequently, England and France both sent permanent ambassadors to The Hague, and the Dutch began to test their new-found position in world affairs. In 1616 the United Provinces offered support to the Duke of Savoy in his dispute with Spain and this conflict might have reopened in the Low Countries if the Pope had not successfully intervened. A similar situation which arose when the Dutch supported Venice was only saved by diplomacy. Meanwhile the Spanish

Firenze, Gall. Pitti

The effects of war
(above) Rubens' allegory on the destruction of war had a personal relevance. As ambassador, the artist had tried to reconcile warring Spain and the Netherlands.

Dutch whalers in a storm
(left) Whaling was an important source of income for the Dutch, who relied on profits from trade to subsidise their rebellion against Spanish rule.

A mercantile power
(below) Dutch economic strength was founded on maritime trade. The merchant fleet grew from around 400 ships in 1532 to over 2500 vessels a century later.

Verbeek/Dutch Merchantman in a Storm with a Whale/National Maritime Museum

A. van de Venne/Middelburg Harbour/Rijkmuseum, Amsterdam

Prince Maurice of Nassau
(left) The cause of Dutch Independence was greatly helped by the military genius of Prince Maurice of Nassau. During the 1590s his army gradually forced the Spanish to withdraw from Dutch territory.

Civic pride
(above) Work on Amsterdam's new Town Hall – seen here from one of the canals – was begun in 1648, the year that the Treaty of Munster was signed. The treaty amounted to a final recognition of Dutch independence, and the Town Hall became a symbol of Amsterdam's civic pride and her important place in the new Dutch nation.

diverted much of their New World silver to defend their colonies, particularly the Philippines, against Dutch naval attack. As the Englishman Owen Feltham wrote a few years later of the Dutch: 'They are the little swordfish pricking the bellies of the Whale'. The slow-moving Spanish Whale seemed an increasingly easy target.

War was resumed in 1621. In the United Provinces, the peace party of Johan van Oldenbarnevelt had been routed and its leader executed: in Spain, colonial power had become the greatest issue, no longer was religion a great motivating force. Thus the war was predominantly an economic struggle, while the military and naval stalemate was occasionally enlivened by significant victories. Again the Spanish placed embargoes on Dutch trade; ironically the Dutch merchants responded by profiting from supplying the Spanish army in the southern Netherlands that their government was fighting. The Dutch navy continued to prick the Spanish colonial belly, and in 1624 seized parts of Portuguese Brazil, though only to lose them the following year.

DUTCH RETALIATION

Meanwhile Spain enjoyed two victories over the Dutch. In 1625 Spanish troops captured the prestigious town of Breda, and in the following year the Spanish fleet beat the Dutch off Gibraltar. The Dutch retaliated by forming an alliance with England and Denmark against the Habsburgs' German interests, which effectively diverted Spain's attention to Denmark. In this period the Dutch also seized the Spanish treasure fleet – a

serious blow to an Empire continually facing bankruptcy. Throughout the 1620s the Spanish were anxious for peace (at one point the artist Rubens was an unsuccessful peace envoy between the two countries) but the United Provinces would not agree to the terms, which included a stipulation for greater Dutch religious tolerance.

The United Provinces may have been holding their own against Spain, but to do so meant alliance with France. When the southern

Netherlands showed signs of revolt in the late 1620s, the French supported the rebel cause. There was to be no question of a United Netherlands – if the South was overrun, the land was to be partitioned between France and the United Provinces. But in 1636 the Spanish took the offensive and sent an army into Picardy. However, Spain's resources were so overstretched that such a venture was doomed to failure. By 1639 French armies had cut the land route to Spain and the Dutch had decisively beaten the Spanish fleet in the Battle of the Downs. But the United Provinces were beginning to realize the danger of a powerful France as ally and neighbour. In 1639 Richelieu reduced the French subsidy to The Hague, because the Dutch were not causing enough trouble to employ Spanish resources.

PEACE CONCLUDED

As late as 1644, the bankrupt Spanish army in Flanders attempted to invade France. The victorious French captured towns in the southern Netherlands and this constituted a veiled threat to the United Provinces. But peace negotiations were under way and the Spanish made every effort to detach the United Provinces from French influence. By the Treaty of Munster in 1648, Spain at last fully recognized Dutch independence. Despite secret negotiations by the House of Orange to prolong the war, the Dutch peace faction prevailed.

William II of Orange died suddenly and during the minority of his son, the United Provinces were governed by an uneasy democratic coalition, with Jan de Witt, the Grand Pensionary or chief officer of the province of Holland, playing a guiding role. As the Spanish Empire failed, France loomed as

D. van Delen/Rijksmuseum, Amsterdam

the greater threat to the independent Dutch. The Spanish army in Flanders was financed after 1648 largely by Amsterdam bankers, for it was politicially, if not financially, expedient to have a buffer state between the United Provinces and France. A complete reversal of the Dutch-Spanish conflict was finally brought about by Louis XIV's ambitions to invade the Low Countries. Ironically, in 1674 it was the turn of the Spanish to ally with the Dutch against the might of France. Not only had Spain unreservedly acknowledged the independence of the United Provinces, and been forced to depend on the Dutch to maintain the Spanish Netherlands, but even the Dutch had sought an alliance with their former enemy against France. The wheel had indeed turned.

The States General
(above) The States General was the sovereign voice of the United Provinces, although each state kept its autonomous administration and decisions that affected all the states were referred to referendum. This painting shows the meeting that took place in 1651 when the States General tried to draw up a new constitution for the nation.

A celebration of peace
(left) Peace was finally concluded between the Netherlands and Spain with the signing of the Treaty of Munster in 1648. The St George's Guard in Amsterdam celebrated the event in characteristic style – with a lavish banquet.

Holland's symbol
(right) The lion was the traditional symbol of all the northern and southern Netherlandish provinces in the years before Dutch Independence. In 1648 Nicholas Visscher gave the age-old image an ironic slant when he used it to symbolize the northern province of Holland standing alone.

A Year in the Life 1666

In this year, when Hals died a pauper, Dutch pride and prosperity were at their height. The United Provinces had the better of the war at sea against England, a country whose afflictions included the end of the Great Plague and the terrible Great Fire of London, both graphically described in Samuel Pepys' diary.

By 1666 the United Provinces had become the leading commercial and maritime power in Europe. Dutch prosperity was largely based on trade with her West African and East Indian colonies, from which the Dutch were determined to exclude their English competitors. The war that consequently broke out between the two countries had gone well for the English in June 1665, with a great naval success off Lowestoft. The diarist Samuel Pepys was to record it as 'a greater victory never known in the world'. In the following June, however, this 'great fight' was eclipsed by a Dutch victory in a gruelling four-day battle off the North Foreland. Both fleets suffered severely, but the English came off worse, and the triumphant Dutch brought back six English vessels as prizes, along with 3,000 prisoners. As the Surveyor General of Victualling, Pepys

Four Days Battle
(*right*) *As the English navy had been unable to follow up their victory at the start of the Second Anglo-Dutch War (1665-7), the Dutch spent the year refitting their navy which was brought up to the impressive figure of 84 warships, 13 frigates and 4 fireships while the English fleet numbered about 80. Of these, a third had been detached under Prince Rupert to deal with a rumoured French advance towards the Channel, leaving the Duke of Albermarle to face the Dutch with the remainder of the fleet off North Foreland on 1 June. The first day went badly for the English and by the second an attempt was made to retreat. On 3 June Prince Rupert's squadron rejoined the main force for the fourth and final day.*

National Maritime Museum

Bridgeman Art Gallery

Museum of London

Great Fire
(*left*) *Nearly four-fifths of the total area of London was devastated by the Great Fire which broke out in a bakehouse in Pudding Lane on the night of 2 September 1666. The city was in uproar as people struggled to save possessions, crowding the streets with carts and horses. 'But Lord', commented Samuel Pepys in his famous, personal diary, 'what a sad sight it was to see the whole city almost on fire'.*

was in the forefront of the frantic efforts made to raise money to provision and re-fit a new fleet. He was so successful that in July the English were able to win a victory at the battle of St James' Flight that partly made up for the North Foreland disaster.

DESIRE FOR PEACE

By the end of the year, both sides were ready for peace. On paper the Dutch position was very strong, since they had Louis XIV of France, Denmark and Brandenburg on their side. By contrast England's only ally had been the Bishop of Munster (an independent principality on the eastern border of the United Provinces), who was soon forced to make peace in April. However, outside the Caribbean (where they captured St

Kitts and Antigua), the French did very little. Since King Louis had designs on the Spanish Netherlands, he was happy to see the English and Dutch – the powers most likely to interfere – at odds; but he had nothing to gain from fighting the English.

The Dutch were also weakened by internal dissensions. The government of the country was largely in the hands of the Grand Pensionary, Jan de Witt, but his republican regime was disliked by supporters of the House of Orange, under whom the country had at times seemed about to become a monarchy. Since the House of Orange had close links with the Stuart Kings of England, Orange supporters favoured peace in opposition to De Witt. One such supporter was Seigneur de Buat, who was supposedly assisting the negotiations between the English Secretary of State, Lord Arlington, and De Witt. Secretly, Buat

Private diaries
(left) Samuel Pepys would be surprised to learn that today he is a household name not on account of the high office he held under two monarchs but because of his private diary, kept from 1660 to 1669. Written in a form of shorthand, the six volumes present a vivid picture of his life. Among many incidents recorded for 1666, Pepys mentions his sittings for the portrait illustrated here, his work for the navy office during a period of national crisis and several disagreements with his wife, during a time of 'public wonder and mischief to this nation'.

By Courtesy of The National Portrait Gallery

Versailles

British Library

Champion of the supernatural
(left) In 1666 Joseph Glanvill, a churchman and member of the Royal Society, published his celebrated A Philosophical Endeavour Towards the Defence of the Being of Witches and Apparitions, *or* Saducismus Triumphatus. *It argued that belief in the reality of the supernatural was concomitant with a belief in God.*

Official mistress
(above) The death of his mother, Anne of Austria, in January 1666 finally freed the 28 year old Louis XIV from the burden of maternal strictures. Within a week his mistress of five years, the adoring Louise de La Vallière, appeared at Mass beside the Queen, thus tacitly announcing her role as mâitresse en titre. *A year later her place in the King's affections was to be usurped by the ambitious Madame de Montespan.*

73

was in contact with England and working to build up a pro-Orange party in the United Provinces. A piece of carelessness ruined his schemes: he handed De Witt a note from Arlington that was in fact a secret communication intended for Buat himself. As a result, Buat was arrested and beheaded and his fellow-conspirators fled into exile. An Anglo-Dutch peace was not made until 1667, after the Dutch had utterly humiliated the English by sailing up the River Medway, burning Sheerness and destroying much of the English fleet laid up at Chatham.

England was beset by calamities during this period. In 1665 the plague struck London, eventually killing almost 70,000 city-dwellers. Though largely spent, the disease lingered on into 1666, when it was finally extinguished by the purging flames of the Great Fire of London.

The fire began accidentally in the Pudding Lane bakehouse of Thomas Farriner. It blazed up at about 2am on 2 September and, thanks to a strong, steady east wind, spread rapidly among the mostly wooden houses of London, which were thoroughly dried out after a long drought. For the first two or three days, fire-fighting efforts were poorly organized, and the streets were choked with refugees struggling to carry their belongings to safety. Pepys sent his plate and money to a friend's house at Bethnal Green and dug a pit in the garden to hold his official papers and stores of wine and Parmesan cheese. London Bridge, Old St Paul's, Guildhall, the Royal Exchange, over 80 churches and 13,000 houses were destroyed during the five days of the fire, leaving 100,000 people homeless.

Lauros-Giraudon

Versailles

Advancement of learning

(above) The French Academie des Sciences, which had begun with informal meetings, was founded in 1666 under the patronage of Louis XIV and the watchful eye of his finance minister, Colbert. To their way of thinking, the achievements of the various academies in the fields of science and the arts added to the greater glory of the Sun King. Both had a keen sense of the value of publicity.

Thomas Rampy/Image Bank

Famous tomb

(left) Shah Jehan died at Agra in 1666 and was buried in the Taj Mahal, the vast and exquisite sepulchre built for his wife Mumtaz Mahal some years before. Since 1658 the Mughal Emperor had been a prisoner of his son Aurangazeb who had killed three brothers to seize the throne, demonstrating a ruthlessness not unlike that shown by Shah Jehan to ensure his own succession in 1627.

National Gallery, London

1606-1669

The son of a miller from Leiden, Rembrandt was the greatest of all Dutch painters and a prolific draughtsman and etcher. He lived in a golden age for Dutch art, but whereas most of his contemporaries were specialists, Rembrandt produced virtually every type of subject. It was as a portraitist that he made his name, however. By his late 20s he was the most popular painter in Amsterdam, and happily married to a wealthy bride.

Thereafter his career was clouded by misfortune – his wife, mistress and five of his six children died, and a financial crisis led to his insolvency when he was 50. Throughout his personal troubles he continued to work triumphantly, although many of his contemporaries preferred the slicker painting of his pupils. It was only in the 19th century that Rembrandt became generally recognized as one of the supreme artists of all time.

75

Holland's Supreme Genius

Rembrandt's early success was followed by tragedy and bankruptcy in later life. Yet his work was not diminished by his misfortune, and he produced some of the most powerful pictures ever painted.

Key dates

1606 born in Leiden

1620 enters Leiden University

c.1624-25 studies with Pieter Lastman. Sets up studio in Leiden

1631/2 moves to Amsterdam

1632 paints *Anatomy Lesson of Dr Tulp*

1634 marries Saskia van Uylenburgh

1641 birth of his son Titus

1642 death of Saskia. Paints *The Night Watch*

c.1645 Hendrickje Stoffels enters household

1654 birth of daughter Cornelia

1656 declared insolvent

1661 commissioned to paint *The Syndics* and *The Oath of Julius Civilis*

1663 death of Hendrickje

1668 death of Titus

1669 dies in Amsterdam

Rembrandt Harmenzoon van Rijn was born in Leiden (then spelt Leyden) on 15 July 1606. His father Harmen (Rembrandt's middle name means 'son of Harmen') was a miller and his mother Cornelia was the daughter of a baker. The family took their name from the nearby 'Rijnmill', a mill on the Rijn (a tributary of the Rhine).

At this time Leiden was second only to Amsterdam in size and importance among the towns of the Netherlands, and Rembrandt's family were comfortably off members of the lower middle class. Rembrandt was the eighth of his mother's nine children.

Rembrandt's mother?
(right) This dignified portrait of an old woman was once thought to have been Rembrandt's mother. She was a devout and serious woman as this painting portrays, but at that time, c.1629, she is unlikely to have looked as old as this sitter.

The artist's home town
(below) Rembrandt was born and educated in Leiden, the second largest town in the Netherlands at the time. Its university, which Rembrandt attended, was one of the most respected in Europe.

Although almost nothing is known of Rembrandt's boyhood, it is safe to assume that he was intellectually the brightest of the children, for while his brothers were sent to learn trades, he became a pupil at the Latin School in Leiden when he was about seven. There he must have gained a thorough knowledge of Latin and absorbed the background of classical history and mythology that would later be put to use in his paintings.

By the age of 14, Rembrandt was studying at Leiden University, which was one of the most distinguished in Europe. His stay was short-lived, however, for within a few months he had

The Royal Collection

HARMAN. GERRITS.

The artist's father c.1630
Shortly before his father's death, Rembrandt made this study of the old man. His expression suggests possible blindness – a frequent theme in Rembrandt's later works.

Swanenburgh is an obscure figure and Rembrandt probably learnt little more than the rudiments of his trade from him, for although in the course of his career he painted most subjects, he never tried his hand at either of Swanenburgh's specialities – architectural scenes and views of hell.

A NEW MASTER

None of Rembrandt's work from this stage in his life survives but he is said to have shown so much promise that his father decided to further his career by sending him to Amsterdam to study with a much more significant artist than Swanenburgh – Pieter Lastman, at this time one of the leading painters in the country. Lastman had travelled in Italy as a young man and had come back eager to show off all he had learned there. His paintings were clever, lively and polished, full of vivid gestures and expressions, and he liked to paint historical and mythological subjects in which he could demonstrate his skill in depicting elaborate costumes and exotic details. Rembrandt stayed only six months with him, but Lastman's work had a powerful effect; he inherited his master's love of colourful stories and his earliest surviving paintings are heavily indebted to him in both subject and treatment.

After he left Lastman, Rembrandt may also have spent some time working in the studios of Jan Pynas and Joris van Schooten, but this can only have been briefly, for by 1625 he had set up as an

convinced his parents that his talents were artistic rather than scholarly, so they abandoned their plans for him to become a member of a learned profession and allowed him to be apprenticed to a painter. The decision was no doubt a very reluctant one, for having a lawyer or a civic administrator as a son would have taken them a rung or two up the social ladder.

The earliest source of information we have on Rembrandt is contained in the second edition (1641) of a book called *Beschrijvinge der Stadt Leyden* (Description of the City of Leiden), by Jan Orlers, who was mayor of the city. He tells us that Rembrandt's parents 'took him to the well painting Mr Jacob Isaaxszoon van Swanenburgh in order that he might be taught and educated by him, with whom he remained about three years'.

Rembrandt's master
(above) Rembrandt first went to Amsterdam to study under Pieter Lastman, a Dutch painter known for his biblical, historical and (shown here) mythological scenes.

Dressed for success
(right) Rembrandt's many self-portraits reflect his changing fortunes. Here, in 1629, he portrays himself as an elegant, intelligent man on the threshold of success.

Friend and Collaborator

Jan Lievens (1607-74), Rembrandt's friend and collaborator during his early career, was a remarkably precocious artist, having set up as an independent painter by the age of 13. In fact, the diplomat Constantijn Huygens wrote of the two young painters 'Rembrandt surpasses Lievens in taste and liveliness of feeling, but the latter exceeds the former in a certain imaginative grandeur and boldness of subjects and figures'. But, unlike Rembrandt, Lievens did not fulfil his early promise. He had a successful career, but his later work, although elegant and accomplished, lacked vigour and freshness.

Lievens: Self-Portrait (c.1644)
(left) From 1644 onwards Lievens divided his time between Amsterdam and the Hague, where he was regarded as an accomplished painter and a popular portraitist.

The Raising of Lazarus (1631)
(below) In his earlier work Lievens was a master of understated drama, as we can see here in this powerful representation of Lazarus emerging from the tomb.

National Gallery, London

A permanent home
(below) With the realization that there was a prosperous career to be had in painting portraits, Rembrandt moved to Amsterdam where he could be sure of influential commissions. He worked hard and productively to secure his position as the city's leading portraitist.

A lover's drawing
(right) To commemorate his engagement in 1633 to Saskia, the well-to-do cousin of his friend and associate, Hendrik van Uylenburgh, Rembrandt drew this tender portrait. He used the Renaissance technique of silverpoint to emphasize how preciously he regarded his fiancée.

Spectrum

Brighton Museum and Art Gallery

independent artist in Leiden. There he worked in close association with Jan Lievens who was a year younger than himself. Like Rembrandt, Lievens was a native of Leiden and had studied in Amsterdam with Lastman. They probably shared a studio for a while and their work was sometimes so similar as to cause confusion: an inventory made in 1632 lists a picture as 'done by Rembrandt or Jan Lievens', and there is a portrait of a child in the Rijksmuseum in Amsterdam signed 'Rembrandt geretucee. . .Lieve. . .' (Lievens retouched by Rembrandt).

The two young artists soon established reputations as major talents in the making. On 14 February 1628, Rembrandt – still only 21 – took on his first pupil, Gerard Dou, and in that year a visitor from Utrecht, the lawyer Aernout van Buchellm wrote in his notebook 'The Leiden miller's son is greatly praised'. In the following year another visitor to Leiden wrote a much fuller account of Rembrandt in his formative years. This was Constantijn Huygens, secretary to the head of state, Prince Frederik Henry of Orange, and one of the most remarkable men of his time. A diplomat and polylingual scholar (he translated John Donne's poems into Dutch), he was also passionately interested in the arts and would have

Kupferstichkabinett, Staatliche Museen Preussischer Kulturbesitz Berlin (West)

Thomas de Keyser/Portrait of Constantijn Huygens and his Secretary/National Gallery, London

become a painter himself but for parental disapproval. Huygens called on Rembrandt and Lievens (the latter had painted his portrait two years earlier) and praised both of them highly. He suggested they should visit Italy, 'for if they become familiar with Raphael and Michelangelo, they would reach the height of painting.' But the two artists said they had no time to travel and that they could in any case see plenty of good Italian paintings in Holland.

SUCCESS AS A PORTRAIT PAINTER

Although he painted (and etched) several portraits of himself and members of his family during his Leiden period, Rembrandt concentrated on figure paintings, notably ones of old men depicted as biblical characters or philosophers, and it was not until 1631 that he is known to have produced his first formal commissioned portrait. This was of the rich Amsterdam merchant Nicolaes Ruts. Rembrandt must have realized that in such works he had a recipe for success, for in late 1631 or early 1632 he moved to Amsterdam and during the next few years devoted himself almost exclusively to portraiture. He moved into the home of the picture dealer van Uylenburgh, with whom he had had business dealings while he was still living in Leiden, and very rapidly became the city's leading portraitist. There were other talented portrait painters working there, notably Thomas de Keyser, but Rembrandt could match them in delicacy of painting costumes and glossiness of finish, and far outstripped them in capturing on canvas a sense of life and personality.

Rembrandt worked with enormous energy in his early days in Amsterdam to consolidate his success. About 50 of his surviving paintings are dated 1632 or 1633 (almost all of them portraits) and even without allowing for the ones that must have disappeared over the centuries, that is a prodigious output. His most famous painting from this time is undoubtedly *The Anatomy Lesson of Dr Tulp* (p.84), which more than any other work showed how far he was ahead of his rivals. Such group portraits were very popular in the Netherlands, and it was a hard task for the painter to bring together a group of virtually identically dressed men without making the picture look rather like a school photograph. Rembrandt's brilliantly arranged group showed the originality of his mind and his superb painterly skills. In 1634, Rembrandt, then 28, married Saskia van

An influential patron
(above) Rembrandt first met the statesman Constantijn Huygens in Leiden. Then, when the artist moved to Amsterdam, Huygens became his most influential patron, procuring commissions from Frederik Henry, Prince of Orange, for whom he acted as private secretary.

Uylenburgh, the 21-year-old cousin of his picture-dealer associate. Saskia was not only from a higher social class than Rembrandt but also fairly well off as she was an orphan and had been left money by her parents. The couple lived with her cousin Hendrik van Uylenburgh for a while and then rented a house on the fashionable Niewe Doelenstraat. We have no first-hand accounts of Rembrandt's relationship with Saskia, but they are hardly necessary, for it was obvious from his paintings and drawings that he worshipped her. Unfortunately their happiness was marred by a succession of infant deaths; between 1635 and 1640 Saskia gave birth to a boy (Rumbartus) and two girls (both named Cornelia after Rembrandt's mother), but none lived longer than two months. Saskia had never been robust and the repeated ordeal weakened her considerably.

Although he had these domestic worries to contend with, Rembrandt's material fortunes were never greater than in the second half of the 1630s. He had all the pupils and commissions he could handle. Writing 50 years after his death, the Dutch painter and historian Arnold Houbracken said that clients had to beg him for pictures and the large sums he was earning enabled him to indulge his passion for collecting. He bought not only paintings, drawings and engravings, but also arms and armour, medals, old costumes, indeed anything that took his fancy or that he thought might come in useful as a prop.

CHANGING FORTUNES

The direction of Rembrandt's career changed in the 1640s. He virtually gave up the type of formal portrait with which he had made his reputation (although he still painted people he knew) and religious paintings began to occupy a correspondingly greater part in his work, which became less flamboyant and more introspective. Various reasons have been suggested to explain this change. The deaths of his mother in 1640 and Saskia in 1642 must have upset him deeply and he may well have found solace in religion. At the same time the pupils he had taught so well were beginning to take some of his market in fashionable portraiture. There may be something in both these ideas, but it is more likely that Rembrandt had simply had enough of routine portraiture and wanted to get back to his first love, which was painting stories from the Bible.

The year before Saskia died she had given birth to a son, Titus, the only one of her four children to survive to adulthood. A woman called Geertge Dircx, the widow of a trumpeter, was hired as the baby's nurse, and after Saskia's death she became Rembrandt's mistress. When she was replaced in his affections by Hendrickje Stoffels, a servant who had entered his household in about 1645, Geertge left and sued Rembrandt for breach of promise. After some unsavoury legal action, Rembrandt managed to get her shut up in an asylum in Gouda, where she remained for five

Rembrandt's Graphic Work

Rembrandt was enormously prolific as a draughtsman and etcher as well as a painter. Most of his drawings are completely private works and many of them seem to be totally spontaneous reactions to the things he saw around him. Unlike the paintings and etchings, very few of the drawings are dated but they give an intimate insight into Rembrandt's mastery.

British Museum, London

Study of a pig
(above) Rembrandt rarely painted animals but he often drew them whether they were unusual, or commonplace like this pig.

Woman Carrying a Child Downstairs
(left) This drawing probably dates from the 1630s and so may well represent Rembrandt's wife, Saskia, carrying one of their children.

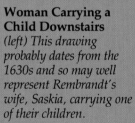

Réunion des Musées Nationaux

Pierpont Morgan Library, New York

Studies of Heads and Figures
(left) These rapid sketches show Rembrandt's ability to convey quirks of gesture and expression.

Sleeping woman
(above) Rembrandt never surpassed the technical bravura of this drawing, which may represent his mistress Hendrickje.

The Omval
(right) The Omval was the name given to a group of houses on a strip of land near the river in Amsterdam. Rembrandt knew it well and made this etching in 1645.

The Singel Canal, Amersfoort
(below) Rembrandt seems to have rarely left Amsterdam, but he made this drawing on a trip to eastern Holland.

Portrait of Titus
The only child of Rembrandt and Saskia to survive infancy was a son called Titus. He became an artist himself and also acted as his father's dealer.

years. It was in the 1640s that Rembrandt began to take a great interest in landscape, and it has been suggested that the walks in the country gave him a welcome rest from his domestic troubles.

Hendrickje, who was about 20 years younger than Rembrandt, remained with him until she died in 1663, and Rembrandt's portrayals of her are as tender and loving as those of Saskia. But, because of a clause in Saskia's will according to which Rembrandt would forfeit his share of her estate if he remarried, he was unable to legalize his relationship with Hendrickje. This got her into trouble with church authorities, who forbade her to take communion because she was living in sin. In 1652 she had a baby who soon died, but in 1654 she gave birth to a girl, called Cornelia as Saskia's daughters had been, who was to be the only one of Rembrandt's children to outlive him.

Now that he was no longer earning a small fortune with his portraits, Rembrandt had difficulty in keeping up the payment on his expensive house, and in the early 1650s his

The Town Hall Controversy

Amsterdam Town Hall, begun in 1648, was the greatest building erected in Holland in the 17th century, a symbol of the city's prestige in its finest period. It was richly decorated with paintings and sculpture by several of the leading Dutch artists of the day. In 1661, Rembrandt received a commission (taking over from a former pupil, Govert Flinck, who had died the previous year) to paint the Oath of Julius Civilis, a subject from ancient history. Rembrandt's painting was installed in 1662, but for unknown reasons was removed the following year – possibly because of the crude realism in the portrayal of Julius – and replaced with a picture by another ex-pupil, Juriaen Ovens.

Commemorative medal
(above) A gold commemorative medal, bearing an image of the classically styled Town Hall, marked its dedication in 1655.

Original plan
(left) Rembrandt's ink and wash preliminary study for the controversial painting gives some indication of the original size of the work – it measured about 18ft. When it was taken down after a year, it is said that Rembrandt cut it down to its present size himself, probably to make it easier to sell.

An appropriate choice
(above) The theme of the painting was chosen because it tells the story of how the one-eyed Julius Civilis assembled the leaders of the Batavians (the original inhabitants of Holland) one night and made them swear to rise against the occupying Romans. The parallel with the Dutch struggle for Independence from Spain, granted in 1648, was obvious.

Living in style
(left) At the height of his career Rembrandt bought a grand house on St Anthoniesbreestraat, a fashionable street in Amsterdam. But during the 21 years he lived there, it became the scene of personal tragedy: his wife and three of his children died there, and eventually, financial difficulties forced him to move. The house is now a Rembrandt museum.

Final years
(below) Rembrandt's enigmatic expression in this self-portrait, painted in 1669, the year of his death, reveals a man who learned to accept, without defeat or bitterness, all the blows life dealt him.

making a fresh start, for his output surged and in 1661 he produced more dated paintings than in any year since the early 1630s.

But despite his renewed success, and foreign acclaim, there was much personal sadness in Rembrandt's final years. Hendrickje died in 1663 and his beloved son, Titus, followed her in 1668. Titus had married in that year and his wife gave birth to Rembrandt's granddaughter, Titia, in March 1669. Rembrandt lived out his final days with his daughter Cornelia and an old servant woman. He lived simply and Houbracken said he was 'often content with some bread and cheese or pickled herrings as his whole meal'. We have only the evidence of the paintings to go on, particularly the self-portraits, but from them it appears that Rembrandt faced his hardships with dignity and no trace of bitterness. His work continued to grow in freedom of technique and depth of expression to the very end of his life, and his late masterpieces take their place among the greatest works of art ever created. He died on 4 October 1669, aged 63, and was buried beside Hendrickje and Titus in the Westerkerk four days later. Cornelia married a painter, Cornelius Suythof, in the following year, and had two children whom she named Rembrandt and Hendrickje.

financial troubles became acute, as he took out one loan to pay off another. He began selling parts of his collections at auction, but more drastic action was called for, and in 1656 he transferred ownership of the house to Titus and was declared insolvent. To avoid the degradation of bankruptcy he applied for and was granted a *cessio bonorum*, a legal procedure which involved the sale of debtor's goods but which allowed him to retain considerable freedom provided he could convince the court of his honesty and good faith. Rembrandt's collections were finally dispersed in two auctions in 1657 and 1658, and in the latter year his house was sold, although he was not forced to move out until the end of 1660. To protect him from his creditors, Hendrickje and Titus formed a business partnership, with Rembrandt technically their employee; in this way he was able to keep the earnings from his work.

THE FINAL YEARS

According to the romantic image of Rembrandt beloved of novelists and film makers, the artist became a pauper and a recluse in his final years. Although it is true that he was never again free from financial worries, this picture is a grave distortion of the truth. Certainly he lived more modestly in lodgings on the Rozengracht, which was in a poorer district on the other side of the city from his house on St Anthoniesbreestraat, and Houbracken tells us that 'in the autumn of his life he kept company mainly with common people and such as practised art', but he was anything but forgotten. The move may in fact have given the artist renewed energy, with the feeling that he was

The Compassionate Eye

A brilliant and versatile artist, Rembrandt painted a wide variety of themes during his career, but it is his compassionate handling of his subjects which give his works their universal appeal.

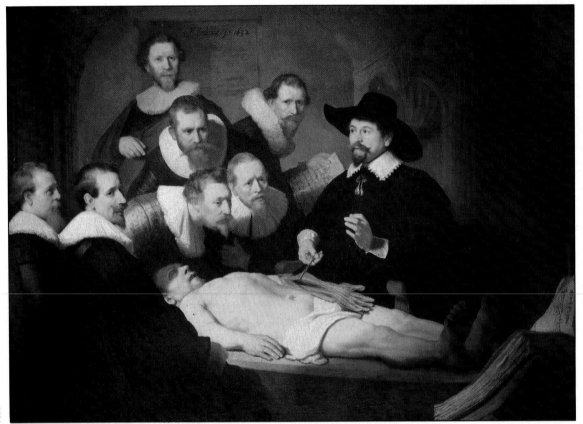

Scala

Mauritshuis, The Hague

The Anatomy Lesson of Doctor Tulp (1632)
(left) Rembrandt's first large painting was commissioned by Nicolaes Tulp, a prominent Amsterdam physician. The painting revolutionized the traditional concept of the group portrait and established Rembrandt's reputation as a portrait painter.

Belshazzar's Feast
(below) One of the many religious works which Rembrandt painted in his lifetime, Belshazzar's Feast *(c.1635) is painted in an extravagant Baroque style, and shows the artist's debt to Caravaggio and Lastman. The subject, taken from the Book of Daniel, is depicted by Rembrandt in a dramatic, almost theatrical manner.*

Rembrandt stands apart from all other 17th-century Dutch artists not only because of the quality of his work, but also on account of its range. The amount of painting produced in Holland in Rembrandt's period was huge, for the country was prosperous and democratic, and pictures were not the preserve of the rich and privileged as they were in aristocratic cultures. Most paintings were produced by specialists, who often worked in restricted fields. Some confined themselves not just to landscapes, but to winter landscapes or dune landscapes, not just to still-life in general, but paintings of fish or flowers. Although Rembrandt excelled at portraits and religious scenes, he painted most subjects in the course of his career, including some, such as *The Polish Rider*, that defy classification.

He not only painted them, but etched and drew them also, for he was a superlative etcher (few would deny that he was the greatest ever master of the technique) and a prolific and brilliant draughtsman. Although scholars disagree on the exact extent of Rembrandt's output (some being more cautious than others as to whether certain works should be attributed to the master himself or to his pupils and imitators), the number of his surviving paintings is usually put at over 500, his etchings at around 300 and his drawings at well over 1000. In all three fields Rembrandt evolved a highly original style and technique.

THE NETHERLANDISH INFLUENCE

As a painter, he began working in the detailed manner that was part of his heritage and stemmed ultimately from the innovations in oil painting of Jan van Eyck. His commissioned portraits of the 1630s, such as *The Anatomy Lesson of Dr Tulp*, are the best examples of the clarity and polish of his early work, but even in his most formal pictures his brushwork is never laboured or finicky. In his more personal work of the same period, particularly self-portraits and portraits of his family, he allowed himself more freedom, often applying the paint quite thickly, and even using the handle of the brush to scrape through it.

National Gallery, London

When, in the 1640s, he began to paint more to please himself than to satisfy his customers, his style became much broader, his brushwork suggesting form and texture rather than minutely delineating it, and in the 1650s and 1660s his *impasto* (thickly applied paint) was one of the most remarkable features of his work. Rembrandt's biographer, Houbraken, wrote that 'in the last years of his life, he worked so fast that his pictures, when examined from close by, looked as if they had been daubed with a bricklayer's trowel' and went on to record that 'it is said he once painted a portrait in which the colours were so heavily loaded that you could lift it from the floor by the nose.' Houbraken's comments are colourful but

A rare oil sketch
(above) This small, but poignant oil sketch of The Entombment of Christ *may be a study for one of a series of paintings on the Passion, executed for Prince Frederik Henry of Orange. Unlike many of his contemporaries, Rembrandt rarely made oil studies for larger paintings, preferring to rework the subject on the canvas itself.*

Penetrating portraits
(above) During the 1630s Rembrandt painted over 65 portraits. This painting of Agatha Bas, the wife of a wealthy Amsterdam merchant, dates from 1641 and is more penetrating than many earlier works. The intense gaze and the beautifully observed detail of the lace, the embroidered bodice and the fan make the portrait particularly memorable.

Dutch landscapes
(below) Rembrandt developed a new interest in landscape at the end of the 1630s and for 15 years produced numerous drawings and etchings of the countryside around Amsterdam. One of the finest examples of his landscape prints is The Three Trees, *which shows his wonderful ability to convey both atmosphere and space.*

exaggerated, and a better notion of the wonderful richness and total expressive mastery of Rembrandt's technique is perhaps conveyed in the celebrated remark of the German Impressionist painter, Max Liebermann: 'Whenever I see Frans Hals [Rembrandt's greatest predecessor in Dutch portraiture], I feel like painting, but when I see a Rembrandt, I feel like giving up!'

Rembrandt's etchings and drawings show equal mastery. At times he used the etching needle as fluently as if it were a pen, but at others he reworked the copper plate again and again to produce an effect of sonorous richness. His drawings, especially those of his mature years, were done mainly with a thick reed pen and were usually self-sufficient works. With a few quick strokes he could bring an animal to life, convey the drama of a biblical story or suggest the airy breadth of the Dutch countryside.

Rembrandt's greatness, however, lies not only in his unsurpassed technical skills, but also in the emotional range and depth of his work. Although very little is recorded of his personal life, his marvellous series of self-portraits gives us the feeling that we know him more intimately than any other great artist.

This remarkable sense of human sympathy

British Museum, London

Group Portraits

The group portrait is a singularly Dutch tradition which originated during the 16th century in response to a demand from officers of guilds, militia companies and charitable organizations for paintings to decorate the walls of their meeting houses. On occasions the picture included as many as 20 people, each of whom contributed towards the painter's fee, but the compositions were generally static, with the sitters arranged in rows or crescents. This convention, broken by Rembrandt's highly original group portraits, is evident in works by his contemporaries Thomas de Keyser and Frans Hals.

Frans Halsmuseum, Haarlem

Stedelijk Museum, Amsterdam

Thomas de Keyser
(1596/7-1667)
The Anatomy Lesson of Dr Sebastian Egbertsz
(left) Thomas de Keyser was the leading portraitist in Amsterdam before Rembrandt's arrival in the winter of 1631/32. This group portrait from 1619 celebrates the anatomy lesson given by Dr Egbertsz in the conventional way, with a series of posed portraits of fellow surgeons arranged symetrically around a central skeleton.

Frans Hals
(1581/5-1666)
Lady Governors of the Old Men's Home at Haarlem
(above) One of the most celebrated portraitists in 17th-century Dutch art, Frans Hals spent his entire career in Haarlem. This dignified painting dates from the end of his life and, although it lacks the dynamic vitality and jovial humour of some of his earlier and best known group portraits of civic guards, shows a deeper understanding of character and age.

TRADEMARKS

Strong Frontal Lighting

In many of his works Rembrandt uses strong frontal lighting to focus the viewer's attention on the main feature of the picture. In the case of portraits it highlights the sitter's face and helps to create the mood.

Barry Thorpe

The Three Crosses
(left) *A supreme master of the etching technique, Rembrandt used a variety of tools to give rich pictorial effects. One of his most dramatic religious etchings,* The Three Crosses *was reworked after 10 years to give an even more powerful, mystical image.*

Portrait of Jan Six (1654)
(below and detail right) *In this painting of his friend and patron, Rembrandt created one of his most impressive portraits. The low viewpoint and dark shadows suggest a forceful presence, while the vigorous brushwork gives spontaneity.*

Six Collection, Amsterdam

extends to his other work, whether he was painting imaginary scenes or portraying the people he saw around him, from rich businessmen to hapless beggars. Although he avidly collected the art of the past and learned greatly from its example, contemporaries were struck by how directly he observed what he saw. The poet Andries Pels, for example, wrote in 1681: 'If he painted, as sometimes would happen, a nude woman,/ He chose no Greek Venus as his model,/ But rather a washerwoman. . ./ Flabby breasts,/ Ill-shaped hands, nay, the traces of the lacings/ Of the corselets on the stomach, of the garters on the legs,/ Must be visible, if Nature was to get her due.' This was not praise, for it was felt that Rembrandt had wasted his talent on lowly subjects.

A REAPPRAISAL

This attitude towards Rembrandt prevailed throughout the 18th century. Although he had many admirers and most critics admitted he was unsurpassed in his mastery of light and shade, he was generally considered to be vulgar. The real change in his critical fortunes came in the Romantic period, with the idea that an artist should express his innermost feelings and flout conventions. In 1851 Delacroix expressed the opinion that Rembrandt would one day be considered a greater painter than Raphael – 'a piece of blasphemy that will make every good academician's hair stand on end.' His prediction came true within 50 years, however, and now when we look for an artist with whom Rembrandt can be compared in breadth and depth of feeling, we turn not to another painter but to Shakespeare.

THE MAKING OF A MASTERPIECE

The Night Watch

Rembrandt's most famous painting – a masterpiece of Baroque complexity – was completed in 1642, the year of Saskia's death. Known somewhat erroneously since the late 18th century as *The Night Watch*, its original title was *The Militia Company of Captain Banning Cocq*, and the subject is the company 'marching out' in daylight – as cleaning in 1946-7 revealed.

Militia companies such as the Kloveniers Company, who commissioned the painting in 1640, had been formed in the 16th century to protect Dutch cities from the Spanish during the War of Independence. In Rembrandt's time their role was mainly ceremonial, and the need for the Watch had long since disappeared, but by showing the company in action, Rembrandt created a work of unprecedented vigour. The painting remained in the Kloveniersdoelen (the Musketeers' Assembly Hall) in Amsterdam until 1715, when it was moved to the Town Hall.

The central figures
(left) Captain Frans Banning Cocq (in black with red sash) orders his Lieutenant, Willem van Ruytenburch (in yellow with ceremonial lance) to march the company out. Both figures are lit by a shaft of light which falls from the top left of the painting, creating the shadow of the Captain's left hand.

A little enigma
(right) The presence of the little girl, so prominent in the painting, has prompted much debate. She may be a symbolic device – the dead fowl at her waist alluding to the Captain's name, or to a shooting match the company may be about to take part in – or simply a means of balancing colours in the painting.

A watercolour copy
(above) Captain Cocq was apparently so pleased with Rembrandt's picture, that he commissioned a watercolour copy for his family album. The copy includes slightly more than the present painting, which lost some 24" (and two background figures) from the left-hand side and smaller amounts from the other three edges when moved to the Town Hall.

The Kloveniersdoelen
(above) The Musketeers' Assembly Hall was an impressive building set back from the edge of the Nieuwe Doelenstraat, where Rembrandt also lived. Between 1639 and 1645 it was decorated with 8 group portraits.

Contrasting styles
(left) The Company of Captain Roelof Bicker was painted for the Doelen by Bartholomeus van der Helst in 1639. A conventional composition, it illustrates the revolutionary nature of Rembrandt's painting.

Gallery

Rembrandt was a prolific artist, painting virtually every type of subject then known, and his imaginative and creative powers were so great that he often crossed the boundaries of conventional categories. The Self-Portrait with Saskia, for example, is primarily a representation of the painter and his wife, but it may also have a religious

Self-Portrait with Saskia
c.1635
64" × 52" Dresden,
Gemäldegalerie

This exuberant work was probably painted soon after Rembrandt's marriage to Saskia when his career was at its most buoyant and his personal life at its happiest. It is generally thought that the picture is not a straightforward portrait, but is meant to have some moralizing intention. Several scholars consider that Rembrandt has here represented himself as the Prodigal Son, who 'took his journey into a far country, and there wasted his substance with riotous living' (Luke 15:13) and who is often shown in a tavern or brothel setting.

significance, and his paintings of the goddess Flora and the biblical character Bathsheba are also portraits of his wife and mistress. Aristotle Contemplating a Bust of Homer and Woman Bathing in a Stream could perhaps be classified as history painting and genre respectively, but they are both of an unusual and highly personal type.

Even when working in the well-established Dutch tradition of group portraiture, Rembrandt found bold new solutions to the old compositional problems in The Night Watch and The Syndics, and in his individual portraits, not least his self-portraits, he was as varied in conception as he was penetrating in characterization.

Saskia as Flora *1635*
48½″ × 38½″ National Gallery, London

Rembrandt painted several pictures of Saskia of a similar type – he obviously loved dressing her up in beautiful costumes. The subject matter of the picture has been much discussed, some scholars thinking that it may represent Proserpine, daughter of the corn goddess Ceres, but the emphasis on flowers is so strong that there seems little doubt that Saskia represents the floral goddess. Such Arcadian subjects were enjoying a great vogue in Holland at this time, following the popularity of the play Granida *(1605) by Pieter Hooft, in which two lovers live an idyllic life in the woods.*

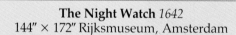

The Night Watch *1642*
144″ × 172″ Rijksmuseum, Amsterdam

This is Rembrandt's largest surviving painting and without doubt his most famous and most discussed work, having had several books and countless articles devoted to it. It has been subjected to much learned (and sometimes fanciful) interpretation, and it has been proposed, for example, that it represents an allegory of the triumph of Amsterdam, inspired by a drama by the great Dutch writer Joost van den Vondel, a contemporary of Rembrandt. The grandeur of the portrayal might seem to invite such high-flown interpretations, but they run contrary to Rembrandt's whole approach to art, and it is more sensible to see the painting as part of the Dutch tradition of civic grand portraits. It was a revolutionary step in that tradition, however, for no previous artist had made such a pictorial drama out of what was a commonplace event. Rembrandt's pupil, Samuel van Hoogstraten, wrote 'It is so painter-like in thought, so dashing in movement, and so powerful' that the pictures hanging alongside it seemed 'like playing cards'. It also marked the swansong of the militia portrait for they went out of fashion soon after this, particularly when the Netherlands had formally achieved independence from Spain in 1648 and there was less of an excuse for the militia to play at soldiers.

Archiv für Kunst und Geschichte

Aristotle Contemplating a Bust of Homer *1653*
55¾″ × 52″ Metropolitan Museum, New York

*This is one of three paintings of famous figures of antiquity that
Rembrandt painted for the Sicilian nobleman Don Antonio Ruffo. The
greatest philosopher of the ancient world is shown with his hand on a
bust of the foremost poet of antiquity, evoking a feeling of meditative
solemnity.*

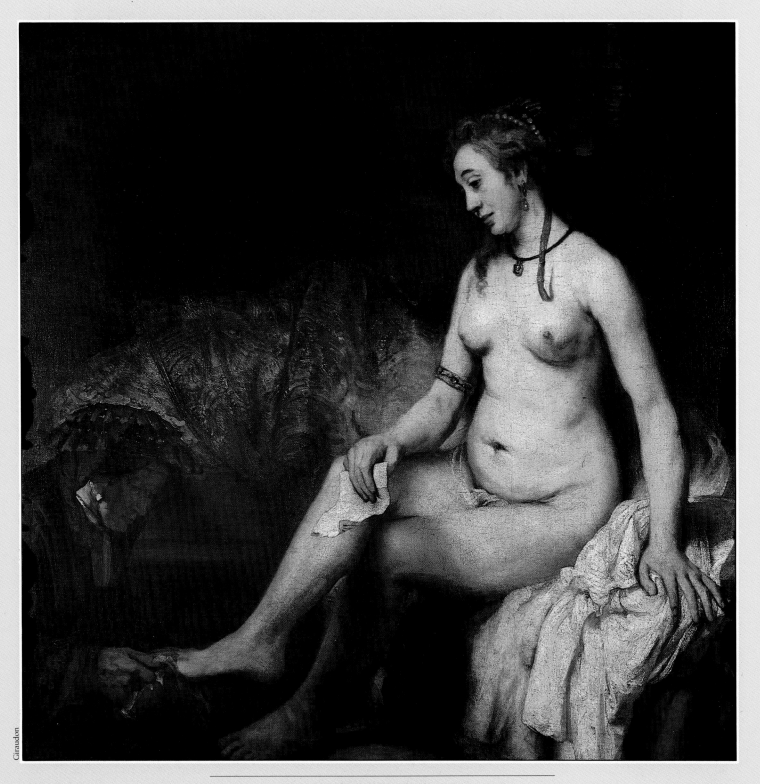

Giraudon

Bathsheba *1654*
56″ × 56″ Louvre, Paris

The model for this painting was probably Hendrickje Stoffels. In the Old Testament, Bathsheba was the wife of a soldier in King David's army. Smitten by her beauty, David had her brought to him and callously seduced her. Rembrandt shows her summonsed by letter, a detail not in the Bible.

A Woman Bathing in a Stream *1655*
24¼″ × 18½″ National Gallery, London

*This small panel is a wonderful example of Rembrandt's individuality
of approach, for it does not fit easily into any of the established
categories of painting and the sensuous brushwork is so bold that it was
very likely painted for his own satisfaction alone. The model
was probably Hendrickje Stoffels.*

Self-Portrait *1658*
51½″ × 40″ Frick Collection, New York

*Rembrandt's self-portraits cover an enormous psychological range.
Often he shows himself at work, but here he has the air of a grand
dignitary holding a cane (a symbol of authority) rather than brushes or
a palette. In fact, his pose and expression recall images of enthroned
kings, and the rich colouring enhances the regal effect.*

The Syndics of the Amsterdam Cloth Workers' Guild 1661-62
75½″ × 110″ Rijksmuseum, Amsterdam

This work is ranked by most critics among Rembrandt's greatest masterpieces. X-rays show that he experimented with the positioning of the figures before finalizing them.

The Jewish Bride c.1665
48″ × 65½″ Rijksmuseum, Amsterdam

Whether this painting is simply a double portrait or, as some critics think, a biblical subject (Isaac and Rebecca?), it is one of Rembrandt's most glorious achievements as a colourist.

Commercial Amsterdam

In Rembrandt's time, Amsterdam was the bustling commercial centre of Europe. Its warehouses were filled with saleable goods and its famous Stock Exchange hummed with profitable activity.

was collected, stored, sold and re-sold. Ships were crammed into its harbour like sardines in a can; loaded lighters (open boats which carried cargo from the quays to the ships) plied up and down the canals; its vast warehouses bulged with goods that had been bought cheaply and would be sold when the price was right; and its markets and stock exchange bustled with the affairs of businessmen from all over the world.

The most significant commodity handled by Amsterdam was money: permission to export monetary metals was rare in the 17th century and the Dutch Exchange Bank (founded in 1609) enjoyed considerable freedom in this respect. The confidence inspired by this bank encouraged the circulation of bills of exchange as negotiable instruments of credit, thereby creating a very modern background for the enterprising 17th-century businessman.

The great building of the Amsterdam Stock Exchange was finished in 1631 and some 4,500

Musée Condé, Chantilly/Lauros–Giraudon

J. van der Ulft/Place du Dam à Amsterdam

Rembrandt's Amsterdam was the commercial and cultural capital of the most densely populated and prosperous area in 17th-century Europe. Its affluent citizens marvelled at their flourishing economy but modestly considered that God was simply rewarding them for the sacrifices they had made on behalf of true religion during the long struggle against Spanish occupation. The whole of mainly Protestant Holland had been under Catholic Spain's rule in the 16th century but the Dutch had waged an 80-year-long war of independence and, by the early 17th century (1609), they had established their own republic, the 'United Provinces'.

God's beneficence seemed to be manifest everywhere in thriving Amsterdam, the world's leading marketplace, where every conceivable commodity

Thriving commerce
(above) In this mid 16th-century view of Amsterdam's main square, merchants negotiate and trade in front of the weighhouse and the new Town Hall.

A busy Stock Exchange
(right) Amsterdam's Stock Exchange was the hub of the city's financial activities. Up to 4,500 merchants passed through its noisy, crowded halls every day.

Emanuel de Witte

Willem van der Vorm Foundation/Museum Boymans–van Beuningen, Rotterdam

merchants of every race and creed crowded into it every day. It was an immensely noisy and exciting scene and the speculation reached a degree of sophistication and abstraction that was unparalleled.

Government stocks and prestigious shares in the Dutch East India Company were prime targets for speculators. Through the pooling of funds invested by its stockholders, the East India Company's vast resources enabled it to send ships round the Cape of Good Hope to cruise the Indian Ocean, the Java Sea and the Pacific as far north as Japan, establishing fortified trading posts in scores of islands and coastal enclaves. The risks were great, but so were the profits: by 1650 the Company's stock certificates were returning 500 per cent per year.

A prosperous couple
(right) The silk, brocade and lace in this couple's dress testifies to the comparative luxury enjoyed by some of Amsterdam's richer inhabitants.

Wealth from overseas
(below) Founded in 1602, the Dutch East India Company had outposts all over the East. This picture shows their Bengal headquarters, and Dutch ships on the Ganges.

Pieter Codde

Mauritshuis, The Hague/Scala

Rijksmuseum, Amsterdam

Schuylenburgh van Hendrik

Christies/Bridgeman Art Library

Abraham Storck

The close alliance between Amsterdam's administrative body – the *Vroedschap*, the *Heeren*, or simply the Regents – and the business community made all this expansion manageable. Through the burgomasters, the Regents intervened in every aspect of Amsterdam life, from the supervision of the postal service to the care of orphans and the setting up of institutions that fostered business. The Regents set up the Chamber of Assurance (1598); the East India Company (1602) and the impressively profitable but not quite as spectacular West India Company (1621); the new Stock Exchange (1608); the special Corn Exchange (1616), the Exchange Bank and the Lending Bank (1614). Moreover, such was the commitment of Amsterdam's leaders to freedom of enterprise that they welcomed skilled or moneyed foreigners to their city, regardless of creed (apart from Catholicism).

A TOLERANT SOCIETY

In the interests of trade, the town fathers admitted foreign craftsmen in large numbers, found housing for strangers and offered extra rewards if they introduced new techniques or improved existing ones. Accordingly, Amsterdam was the home of a large Jewish community, many of them refugees from intolerant Portugal and Spain. Through his contacts with Jews – at least 35 of his portraits of them survive – Rembrandt drew inspiration for his depictions of the great figures of the Old Testament from whom they were descended.

Amsterdam harbour
(left) Dutch wealth was based on the overseas trade that passed through Amsterdam harbour. Business boomed as Protestant merchants fled from the rival port of Antwerp following persecution by their Spanish rulers.

To foreigners it seemed a miracle that Amsterdam, once a fishing village, and its marshy hinterland had become the pivot of world trade. 'The art of industry has made a masterpiece of nature's miscarriage' was how one French visitor put it. But in Rembrandt's day the city was refurbished to better fulfil its new status. The 'plan of the three canals', based on a massive land reclamation project, was approved by the Regents and put into effect between 1612 and 1665.

ECONOMIC EXPANSION

Through the use of stakes and cowhides to provide stable foundations, the area within the city's boundaries was extended from 180 to 720 hectares. The new-style Amsterdam acquired its distinctive crescent shape from the three great canals, linked to one another by smaller ones. It was along these canals – the Heerengracht, the Keizersgracht and the Prinsengracht – that the richest citizens had their magnificent houses built, and this period was generally complemented by the first intensive phase of building in brick and stone. The city's population kept pace with its economic take-off and more than justified such expansion.

Amsterdamers were noted for their diligence and efficiency. Travellers commented that there were few vagrants to be seen, largely because charity was not available to the able bodied, and the city was thriving. Everyone seemed to work: children were trained and assisted in family workshops and businesses; old people remained

A city of art lovers
(above) Art dealing flourished in newly rich Amsterdam, and artists were able to sell their works to an expanding art market of middle-class buyers, rather than having to rely on individual aristocratic patrons. As the pictures in this painting show, Dutch artistic taste was quite wide-ranging.

Canal architecture
(left) Wealthy merchants lived in distinctive gabled houses along Amsterdam's three main canals. These waterways – the Heerengracht, the Keizersgracht and the Prinsengracht – were all built during Rembrandt's lifetime.

active as long as they could; and the managerial abilities of the burghers' wives, who often took over their husbands' affairs, testified to the excellent education available to both sexes.

Just as they combined their business affairs with involvement in municipal responsibilities, so the Amsterdamers saw no incompatibility between love of money-making and love of the arts and scholarship. The English distinction between gentlemen and tradesmen did not apply. The writer Pieter Hooft was also a government official and a man of business; the poet Joost van der Vondel a stocking merchant; and the brilliant scientist Anthonie van Leeuwenhoek a conscientious book-keeper.

A NEW ART PUBLIC

The Regents of Amsterdam resisted the Calvinist zealots who continually urged them to crack down on a liberal cultural life and maintained a pragmatic approach. Thus they refused to destroy church organs, allowing them to be used for the secular concerts that they sponsored. In general the new secular elite took over the patronage of the arts to a far greater extent than the Church ever had. In fact, private homes and public buildings now replaced cathedrals and castles as the showhouses for artistic endeavour.

Flemish School/Cognoscenti in a Room Hung With Pictures

National Gallery, London

Serious citizens

(right) De Hooch's painting perfectly conveys the subdued and diligent character of Amsterdam's soberly-dressed inhabitants, who were devout Calvinists, shrewd merchants and responsible citizens.

Just as the Dutch refused to let strict Calvinist dictates impinge on all of their worldly affairs, so they also avoided any ideological constraints on their trading activities – for shrewd Dutch merchants the customer was always right. The warehouses of Amsterdam regularly supplied foreign armies, for example, and not just those of Holland's allies. But such flexibilities meant that the only other Protestant Republic, Cromwell's England, was allowed to become Holland's chief competitor rather than its greatest friend.

The first Anglo-Dutch War (1652-4) broke out when longstanding commercial and colonial rivalries between these two maritime powers were made worse by the English Navigation Act of 1651, which permitted only English ships to serve English colonial ports. This war nearly ruined Amsterdam because Dutch commercial life depended on the passage of the great trading fleets from America, Africa and Asia through the English Channel. In 1653 the port of Amsterdam was under a blockade that lasted for weeks until it was finally broken by Admiral Tromp at a fearful cost in lives and men. The fortunes of artists are always sensitive to national fortunes. It is extremely likely that Rembrandt's sad plight in 1656 owed something to the national disaster that had unnerved many of his potential clients.

Archiv für Kunst und Geschichte

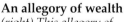

Walther/Victoria & Albert Museum, London

A Dutch obsession

(left) The tulip was introduced to Holland from Turkey in the early 17th century, and rapidly became a national obsession. Enormous sums of money could be made by breeding the striped and variegated species, but when the bottom fell out of the tulip market in 1637, the whole economy felt the effect.

An allegory of wealth

(right) This allegory of wealth – in which Amsterdam personified as a queen accepts gifts from the four continents – forms the frontispiece to a history of the city published in 1663. Printing was an important industry in 17th-century Amsterdam, which had over 40 printing establishments.

A Year in the Life 1655

Rembrandt's old friend Manasseh ben Israel was in London during 1655 arguing for the admission of the Jews to England. Oliver Cromwell was sympathetic, despite his preoccupations with the increasing difficulties of maintaining internal security and continuing overseas expansion at the expense of Catholic Spain.

Rembrandt was neighbour to Manasseh ben Israel, one of the leaders of the Jewish Community in Amsterdam, and was clearly an old acquaintance of his by the time he provided four etchings for Manasseh's book *The Glorious Stone,* published in 1655. Written in Spanish, the scholar argued ingeniously from Scripture that the Messiah would not come until there were Jews in every land and since there were reports that the Lost Tribes had been located in the New World, Manasseh regarded it as a matter of urgency to secure the re-admission of the Jews to England (they had been expelled in 1290).

In September 1655 this pressing need prompted Manasseh to visit London, where he lodged in the Strand and dined with the Lord Protector himself. In October, the formal petition by Manasseh, 'A Divine and a Doctor of Physic on behalf of the

Jamaica conquered

(right) The New Year saw a British naval force under the command of William Penn and Robert Venables on its way to the West Indies to attack Spanish possessions there. An assault on San Domingo (modern Dominican Republic) ended in ignominious defeat but, by May, the British force had succeeded in wresting Jamaica from Spain's grasp.

The British Library

Meier/Zefa

The fall of Cracow
(left) In the autumn of 1655, Cracow – then the capital of Poland – fell to the invading Swedish forces under Charles X, and the Polish King John Casimir fled. Although the Swedes never really subdued the Poles, this victory marked the start of a brilliant, if brief, military career for Charles.

An eminent Jew
(right) In September, Rembrandt's friend and neighbour from Amsterdam, Manasseh ben Israel, set off to London on what he felt was an urgent mission – to persuade Cromwell to admit Jews to England once more. But despite Cromwell's tacit support, the mission achieved only partial success.

Jewish Nation', caused intense controversy. In December, a committee of the Council recommended rejection of the petition, although any action was left to Cromwell's discretion. In practice, unobtrusive Jewish settlement was allowed from this time onwards. But since there was no change in the law, Manasseh believed he had failed. Cromwell's interest in the matter is striking in view of his many preoccupations during 1655. His assumption of the Protectorate backed by a loyal army of two years previously had created enemies in republican ranks in addition to the Royalist supporters of the exiled Charles II. In January, when voices were raised in Parliament against a Militia Bill, Cromwell dissolved it and sent the members home after delivering a long and angry speech. In February a purge of social radicals was completed when one of

their leaders, John Wildman, was arrested as he was dictating a pamphlet against 'the tyrant Cromwell', and in April, Colonel John Penruddock's Royalist insurrection in the West, which had hoped to profit from dissension within republican ranks, failed to gain momentum and was easily put down.

CROMWELL BECOMES A VIRTUAL DICTATOR

Since he could not find an amenable parliament, Cromwell decided to institute a period of direct army rule. The country was divided into eleven districts, each controlled by a major-general who was instructed to control or prohibit all possible seditious assemblies – which included ale-houses, race-meetings, cock-fights and football matches.

The party's over
(above left and above) Faced with growing divisions within republican ranks, Cromwell took power into his own hands, dissolving Parliament in January to rule almost as a military dictator. One of his more unpopular measures was a ban on immoral fun such as drinking.

105

Cromwell was also busy strengthening the navy, which had just triumphed over England's chief maritime rivals, the Dutch. In 1655 the formidable 1000-ton *Naseby* was launched, and a fleet led by England's great admiral, Robert Blake, defeated the Barbary pirates of North Africa and forced the Bey of Tunis to release all the English captives who slaved at the oars of his galleys. An expedition sent out to the West Indies under William Penn and Robert Venables met with more mixed fortunes. Badly prepared and with a divided command, the fleet failed to capture the Spanish colony of Hispaniola (modern Haiti and Dominica). It was more by luck than good judgement, that they were able to seize Jamaica.

Since Spain was still, in English eyes, the leading Catholic power (as well as possessing temptingly rich colonies), it seemed good policy to ally with Spain's enemy in Europe, France. An Anglo-French treaty was thus duly signed in October 1655.

This had two advantages from Cromwell's point of view. The French were forced to expel the exiled Charles II as well as bring pressure to bear on the Duke of Savoy to end the persecution of the Waldensians. The savage repression of this little Protestant sect, which had survived for centuries in the mountain valleys of Piedmont, was the European sensation of 1655. In England the Council proclaimed a fast, huge sums were collected for relief work, and John Milton wrote an angry sonnet which began 'Avenge, O Lord, thy slaughtered saints.' However, Cromwell's more diplomatic solution worked, and today there are still Waldensians in the mountains.

Louvre, Paris/Giraudon

Bartolome Murillo
(1617-1682)
The Birth of the Virgin
(above) This painting, begun in 1655, is an early example of Murillo's break with the naturalistic tradition of Spanish religious art.

A philosophical Leviathan
(left) In 1655 the De Corpore *of the great English philosopher Thomas Hobbes was published.*

St Sulpice, Paris
(right) An example of the French classical style, this elegant church was originally built in 1655.

William Dobson/The Royal Society

Giraudon

I. Ver-Meer

1632-1675

Vermeer is one of the most highly regarded Dutch artists of all time, yet his life remains shrouded in obscurity. As far as we know, he spent all his life in his native town of Delft, where he seems to have worked as an art dealer and run a tavern in order to support his family of 11 children. It is hardly surprising that painting appears to have been a part-time activity, and Vermeer's output was very small.

There are only about 35 authenticated works by Vermeer, but in them the artist perfected a style and approach to painting that were entirely his own. His best-known pictures show interiors with one or two figures reading, writing or playing music, quietly absorbed in their tasks. The colours are always fresh and cool, the paint sparkles with reflected light, and the total image is one of composed serenity.

'The Sphinx of Delft'

**Vermeer was born in Delft and spent all his life in the town.
But although local records give only a few glimpses of his life,
he remains an enigmatic figure, aptly called 'the Sphinx of Delft.'**

Among the many great painters of 17th-century Holland, Vermeer now stands second only to Rembrandt in both popular appeal and scholarly esteem. His pictures rank among the most familiar and best-loved images in world art. However, knowledge of his life is sadly limited because almost all the contemporary references to him are colourless official documents.

Johannes (or Jan) Vermeer was born in Delft and baptized in the town's New Church on 31 October 1632. He was the second of two children (the other was a girl) of Reynier Janszoon and Digna Balthasars; it was only from 1640 that his father Reynier started using the surname Vermeer. At the time of his marriage in 1615 Reynier had given his occupation as silkworker, but he later became an innkeeper and he also dealt in paintings. In 1623 he was almost bankrupt, but he subsequently prospered (perhaps due to his

Early influences
(below and right) Vermeer's father tried his hand at several trades and prospered most from a combination of picture dealing and innkeeping. Both activities seem to have had their influence on Johannes for he soon indulged his taste in art and, after his father's death in 1652, it is assumed that he took charge of the inn.

Jan Steen; Two Kinds of Games/Rijksmuseum, Amsterdam

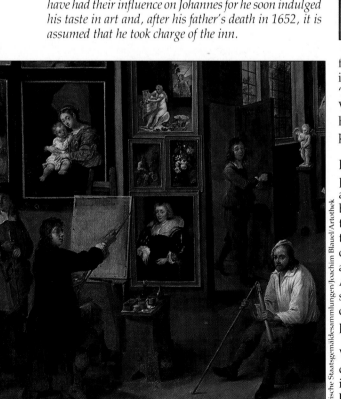

Detail: David Teniers: The Gallery of Archduke Leopold in Brussels

fortunate or skilful dealing in the art market), and in 1641 he bought an inn and a large house called 'Mechelen' in the main square of Delft. The young Vermeer grew up in this tavern, which may have had something of the atmosphere conveyed in the paintings of Brouwer (p.133) and Steen (p.134).

Delft, where Vermeer was to spend his entire life, was then Holland's fourth largest town. It was prosperous and tranquil, with a particularly attractive centre dominated by the medieval buildings and spires that appear in many views of the town painted by Delft artists. The town had a tradition of painting stretching back to the late 15th century, although it had become something of an artistic backwater by the time of Vermeer's birth. Around 1650, however, several talented painters settled in the town, and Vermeer's career coincided with a brief golden period in Delft painting.

It is not known which of the Delft artists Vermeer chose as his master, but with a picture dealer for a father it must have been easy to indulge a taste in art and find a suitable teacher; Leonaert Bramer has often been suggested as a possible candidate. He spent most of his life

Bayerische Staatsgemäldesammlungen/Joachim Blauel/Artothek

Bullaty Lomeo/Image Bank

The artist's wife?
(right) Vermeer married Catharina Bolnes, after some resistance from her mother, in 1653. Catharina possibly modelled for this work in the same year. Despite a modest income, the couple had 11 children.

Key Dates

1632 born in Delft, Holland

1641 father buys inn and house called 'Mechelen'

c.1650 Fabritius moves to Delft

1653 marries Catharina Bolnes; made a master in Delft painters' guild

1654 Delft partially destroyed by an explosion which kills Fabritius

1662-63 made official of Delft's painters' guild

1667-71 reappointed official of painters' guild

1672 visits The Hague

1675 dies in Delft; wife declared bankrupt

Vermeer; Woman in Blue Reading a Letter/Rijksmuseum, Amsterdam

working in Delft, and there is a documented connection between him and Vermeer: it was Bramer who intervened on Vermeer's behalf when his future mother-in-law, Maria Thins, at first refused to sign the marriage contract. Bramer is an interesting minor artist who had travelled in Italy and France, and is remembered mainly for his dramatically lit night scenes. However, there are no similarities between his dark, crowded pictures and Vermeer's paintings, which casts doubt on the idea that he was Vermeer's artistic mentor.

There are more obvious stylistic links between Vermeer's work and that of Carel Fabritius, who had studied with Rembrandt and who moved to

Delft in about 1650. The fact that Fabritius seems to have shared Vermeer's interest in optical experimentation in his paintings further reinforces the suggestion of a connection between the two artists, but in the absence of any documentation, the precise nature of the relationship must remain obscure. Fabritius was killed in the most disastrous event in Delft's history, when the gunpowder magazine exploded in 1654 destroying part of the town. The artist's death led a Delft publisher to compose a memorial poem, the last verse of which mentions Vermeer: 'Thus this Phoenix was extinguished, To our loss, at the height of his power. But happily there arose from his fire Vermeer, who followed in his footsteps with mastery.' Whether or not this implies a master-pupil relationship between the two artists, it shows that they were to some extent linked together in the public mind.

THE ARTIST MARRIES

Vermeer was made a master in the painters' guild on 29 December 1653. Earlier that year he had married Catharina Bolnes. She came from a higher social class, and her mother, who was divorced and wealthy, at first objected to the match. But Bramer and another respected citizen went to see her and persuaded her to change her mind, no doubt assuring her of her future son-in-law's talent and good prospects. Little is known of the details of the marriage. The couple had 11 children and, although they do not appear in Vermeer's paintings, it is quite likely that Catharina served as a model for pictures such as *Woman in Blue Reading a Letter* (above). Catharina was a Catholic, and it is possible that Vermeer was converted to his wife's faith. The *Allegory of Faith*

The artist's home town
(left) In 1632 Johannes Vermeer was born in Delft, then Holland's fourth largest town. He lived there all his life and is only once documented as having made a visit elsewhere.

Delftware
(right) Delft had principally achieved its prosperity by producing a particular type of beautiful glazed earthenware to which the town gave its name.

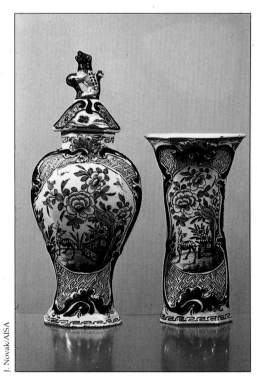

J. Novak/AISA

Carel Fabritius

Carel Fabritius (1622-54) was Rembrandt's most gifted pupil, and one of the few who managed to overcome his overwhelming influence to create a highly personal style. Fabritius settled in Delft in about 1650, and he exerted a profound influence on painting in the town until his life was cut short by the explosion of 1654. His use of a natural daylight atmosphere and luminous tones must have been a revelation to the young Vermeer, and the similarities between their work has led to speculation that Fabritius was Vermeer's master.

Mauritshuis, The Hague

The Goldfinch
(above) This little panel anticipates Vermeer's work in its simplicity and in its use of a dark object placed against a light background for tonal contrast.

Self-Portrait
(left) The broad handling of paint in this portrait shows the influence of Rembrandt, but there is an air of self-possession and confidence in the artist's expression.

National Gallery, London

Delft disaster
(above) In 1654 much of Vermeer's home town was destroyed when a gunpowder magazine exploded. The artist was left unscathed but his possible master, Carel Fabritius, died.

(p.118) symbolizes the Catholic faith in particular, and Vermeer's youngest son had the typically Catholic name of Ignatius.

Vermeer's father had died the year before the marriage, and it is sometimes assumed that the young painter took over the running of the inn. There is no direct evidence for this, but it is not improbable as Vermeer continued to live in 'Mechelen', and he would probably have needed a

Hard times
(left) A few months after Vermeer's death, his wife was declared bankrupt. The invasion of Holland by a French army had caused the art market to collapse, but even before that Vermeer is recorded as having to borrow money and let out his house.

source of income in addition to painting to support his growing family.

It is highly likely that Vermeer took over his father's art business as well. He certainly dealt in paintings and must have had something of a reputation as a connoisseur, for in 1672 he went to The Hague (the only time he is recorded as leaving Delft) to be an 'expert witness' in a dispute concerning the authenticity of a group of Italian paintings. Vermeer gave them short shrift, declaring that they were not only 'no outstanding Italian paintings, but, on the contrary, great pieces of rubbish'.

Vermeer must have been a respected figure among his fellow artists in Delft because in 1662-63, and again in 1670-71, he was a *'hooftman'* ('headman' or governor) of the painters' guild. We know that his pictures were highly prized by some because of the account of Balthasar de Montconys, a French art dealer who visited Delft in 1663: 'I saw the painter Vermeer who did not have any of his works' he wrote in his journal, 'but we did see one at a baker's, for which six hundred livres had been paid, although it contained but a single figure, for

Egbert van der Poel; Conflagration of a Dutch Town at Night/Staatliche Kunsthalle, Karlsruhe

which six pistoles would have been too high a price in my opinion.' Vermeer's pictures were either bought by the humble burghers of Delft, or given to tradesmen to offset family debts. There is also some evidence that Vermeer had a regular patron, Jacob Dissius, who apparently owned 19 of the artist's works in 1682, seven years after the artist's death.

MONEY TROUBLES

In spite of this patronage, Vermeer found himself in financial difficulties. In 1657 he is recorded as borrowing 200 guilden, and in 1672 he rented out his house for 180 guilden a year and moved in with his mother-in-law. Later that year Holland was invaded by a French army, and although the occupying force was soon driven out, the economic crisis that accompanied the trouble caused the art market to collapse. Vermeer's already unstable business affairs collapsed with it. When Vermeer died late in 1675 at the age of 43, he left a large unpaid debt, eight children under age, and a host of financial problems for his widow. A few months after his funeral in Delft's Old Church, Catharina was declared bankrupt.

Vermeer's reputation was entirely eclipsed after his death, and his pictures were often sold at auction as works by masters such as de Hooch and Metsu. It was not until the 19th century that he was rescued from oblivion by the French journalist Theophile Thoré who succeeded in identifying about two thirds of the Vermeers we know today. Thereafter, Vermeer's fame grew quickly, and now all but a handful of Vermeer's authenticated paintings are the prize possessions of the world's greatest galleries, but the artist still remains, as Proust once described him, 'an enigma in an epoch in which nothing resembled or explained him.'

Museum of Fine Arts, Boston (Purchased, Maria T.B. Hopkins Fund)

The Procuress
(above) Vermeer's mother-in-law owned Dirck van Baburen's Procuress (1611). It appears in the backgrounds of two of Vermeer's works (p.113 and p.125).

A pale imitation
(right) Vermeer's work was rediscovered in the 19th century and by the 1920s Van Meegeren was fooling the art market with his forgeries.

Van Meegeren; Woman Reading Music

Pure Harmony

Vermeer produced a small body of work of exceptional beauty and clarity. He is best remembered for his gentle scenes of domestic life, which can, however, often be read on another level.

Tom Scott

National Galleries of Scotland, Edinburgh

Christ in the House of Mary and Martha
(left) This is Vermeer's earliest surviving work and his only painting on a biblical theme. But although the subject-matter is uncharacteristic there are several typical stylistic features: the sensitive treatment of light, the calm, naturalistic poses and the interest in richly patterned textiles.

The Procuress (1656)
(below) This genre work reveals the influence of van Baburen's The Procuress *(p.111), which Vermeer's family owned.*

with his name that even 30 years after his reputation was established by Theophile Thoré, one of them – the signed *Diana and her Companions* – was attributed to an obscure namesake, Jan Vermeer of Utrecht. The only other picture of this type by Vermeer is *Christ in the House of Mary and Martha* (left), but it is possible that other early works were destroyed in the explosion of 1654 in Delft. Both these pictures show the influence of Italian painting with which Vermeer was well acquainted through the family art-dealing business. They were probably painted a year or two before *The Procuress*, his first dated work.

DOMESTIC SCENES

The Procuress (below) provides a transition to the next phase of Vermeer's development, for although – like the history paintings – it is a large-scale work of a warm tonality, it takes its subject from contemporary life, as did virtually all his subsequent pictures. After *The Procuress*, however, Vermeer favoured much quieter subjects, generally involving only one or two figures

Although a few of the pictures attributed to Vermeer are still the subject of scholarly controversy, it is generally agreed that the number of surviving paintings from his hand is not much more than 35. There are good reasons for thinking that the number was never substantially larger than this, for most of the Vermeers mentioned in 17th and early 18th-century sources can be identified with paintings that survive today, and only a few of the paintings now given to him are not mentioned in these sources. It is almost inevitable that in the course of centuries some of Vermeer's work must have accidentally perished, but it is reasonably certain that the majority has survived intact.

DATED WORKS

Vermeer often signed his work, but only three of his 30-odd paintings are dated. *The Procuress* (1656) *The Astronomer* (1668) and *The Geographer* (1669). None of the remainder can be firmly dated on other evidence, so it has proved difficult to construct a convincing chronology for his work. Nevertheless, three broad phases are generally recognized in Vermeer's development. In the first, he painted large-scale history pictures which are so different from the quiet domestic scenes associated

Mauritshuis, The Hague

The Pearl Earring
(above) This fresh and simple portrait is remarkable for its delicacy and immediacy. The lustre of the pearl earring is imparted to the girl's eyes and moist lips.

Preussischer Kulturbesitz, Berlin

Staatliche Museen, Berlin

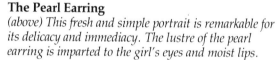

The Pearl Necklace
(above) This is one of Vermeer's most beautiful works, relying on the most subtle of light and colouristic effects. It probably conveys a gentle moral on the theme of worldly vanities.

Lady Seated at the Virginals
(right) This late work forms a pair with the Lady Standing at the Virginals *(p.117). Both are concerned with the relationship between music and love.*

engaged in simple everyday tasks or making music, and his colouring became much cooler. This represents the middle phase of Vermeer's career (into which most of his pictures fall), when he created those gentle images of domestic life that raised genre painting to a level that has never been surpassed. His two celebrated townscape pictures also date from this period of great achievement.

In the final phase of Vermeer's work, many critics discern a certain hardening of style and loss of freshness. He was such a marvellous craftsman that he never painted any picture that does not have passages of great beauty, but the works that are attributed to his final years, when his financial problems were worsening, do seem to lack the utter naturalness of his finest works. Among these later productions is the only one of Vermeer's paintings that is generally considered a

National Gallery, London

conspicuous failure – the *Allegory of Faith* (p.118). The lumbering personification of Faith produces an almost comical effect and it is tempting to imagine that Vermeer took the commission reluctantly, for his talents were totally unsuited to this type of work, which Rubens, for example, did so well. Several of Vermeer's other paintings are imbued with symbolic meaning – seen most obviously in *A Woman Weighing Pearls* – but the *Allegory of Faith* is the only work where symbolism is the primary intention; all the others and make perfect sense on a naturalistic level.

EARLY INFLUENCES

Superficially, Vermeer's genre paintings are very similar to those of many of his Dutch contemporaries. In his early career he was heavily influenced by the works of the Utrecht masters, Baburen, Terbrugghen and Honthorst, who worked in the dramatic style of the Italian artist, Caravaggio. Baburen's *The Procuress* (p.111) appears in the background of two of his works and was clearly one of his favourite paintings. But what sets Vermeer apart from his fellow artists is that he would not settle for anything less than perfection. His best works have a sense of harmony and serenity that lifts them from the sober prose of run-of-the-mill interior scenes to the realms of poetry, and his colouring and brushwork are among the miracles of art.

Vermeer is particularly associated with subtle harmonies of blue, pale yellow and grey, but one of his most remarkable characteristics is his ability to use bright and strongly lit colours without them ever seeming to jar. In *The Lacemaker* (p.130), for example, the three primary colours – blue, red and yellow – are set off boldly against one another. This vibrant blend of colour is enhanced by his masterly brushwork. In reproductions, Vermeer's paintings sometimes look smooth and highly detailed, but in front of the originals one is always aware of the marks of the brush. The paint is often applied quite broadly (in *Maid with a Milk Jug* (opposite) the contrast between highlight and shadow on the woman's left arm brings Manet to mind), and little raised points of paint suggest the play of light on objects in a way that is totally convincing optically and of the utmost delicacy pictorially. The Dutch painter and critic Jan Veth remarked that his paint looks like crushed pearls melted together.

WORKING METHODS

Nothing is known for certain about Vermeer's working methods. No drawings by him are known, so it may well be that he painted directly onto the canvas. This seems to be borne out by the representation of the artist in *The Artist's Studio* (p.118), where the design is indicated on the canvas in progress with a few strokes of light paint and there is no elaborate underpainting. The only other technical point illustrated by this painting (which it is reasonable to assume represents

The Camera Obscura

It has long been thought that Vermeer used a *camera obscura* to help with his compositions. Many characteristics of his work, such as the white dots of paint he frequently employed, and his enlargement of foreground figures, may relate to the optical effects produced by the device. There were two basic types of camera obscura in Vermeer's time: the simplest kind was a darkened room with a small aperture through which light could pass, which was especially useful in composing landscapes; the more developed variety was a smaller box with lenses, which could be used for interior views.

The viewing box
(left) This compact machine would have been useful for assessing perspective in paintings of interiors.

Foreground enlargement
(below) A detail from View of Delft *shows the enlargement of foreground detail typical of the use of the camera obscura.*

Mauritshuis, The Hague

Maid with a Milk Jug

(left and detail above) The tiny specks of light in this painting are like those seen through an unfocused lens. This implies that Vermeer had observed the phenomenon himself.

Rijksmuseum, Amsterdam

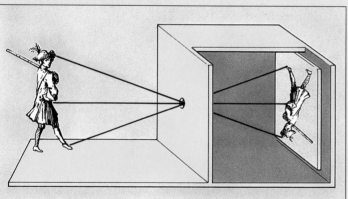

The darkened room

(above) The most simple form of the camera obscura is a darkened room with an aperture. The image is reflected on the wall upside down and reversed.

The portable camera obscura

(below) Here a lens focuses the image, which is reflected by a slanted mirror onto a translucent screen. It is the right way up, but is reversed.

The use of lenses

(above) A diagram dated 1642 demonstrates how lenses could be used to correct an image so that it was reproduced faithfully.

A scientific association?

(left) Anthony van Leeuwenhoeck was working on lenses and microscopes in Delft during Vermeer's lifetime, and it is quite likely that the artist knew of his experiments in optics.

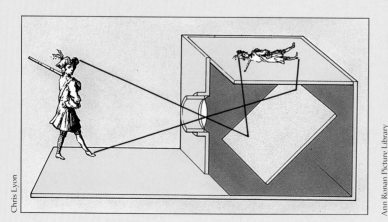

Chris Lyon

Ann Ronan Picture Library

115

Sleeping Girl
(right) *Described in an early auction catalogue as 'a drunken, sleeping young woman at a table', this painting may represent the sin of 'idleness' or 'sloth'. The curious spatial construction with its sloping foreground points to the use of an optical device like the camera obscura.*

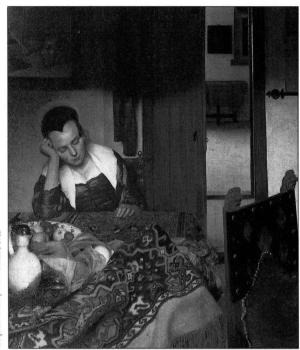

Bequest of Benjamin Altman, 1913

Metropolitan Museum of Art, N.Y.

Vermeer's own practices) is that the artist is using a mahlstick – a stick with a padded knob at one end, which is held against the canvas so the painter can support his right hand when painting detailed passages. Apart from these few technical clues, this work also demonstrates Vermeer's use of popular handbooks like Cesare Ripa's *Iconologia* for standard symbolic details and allegorical attributes – like the sculpted mask symbolizing 'imitation'.

INTEREST IN OPTICS

In spite of the lack of documentary knowledge, most critics have come to the conclusion that Vermeer often made use of a *camera obscura*. This was a device that worked on the same optical principle as the modern photographic camera, but instead of projecting an image by means of a lens onto light-sensitive film, the camera obscura projected it onto a drawing or painting surface, so that the outline of the image could be traced. It was a speedy way of ensuring accuracy for certain types of subjects (it appealed to townscape painters but was of no use to portraitists) and had a

COMPARISONS

The Domestic Interior

Flemish masters of the 15th century often included domestic detail in their religious works, and this observation of everyday life paved the way for 17th-century Dutch genre paintings, which depict domesticity for its own sake. Interest in the humble interior continued into the next century in the work of artists such as Chardin, and culminated in the 19th century with the laundresses, cooks and maids painted by the Impressionists.

Hunterian Art Gallery, University of Glasgow

Jean-Baptiste-Siméon Chardin (1699-1779) The Scullery Maid
(left) *Chardin's solemn interiors with one or two figures going about their business, have a simplicity and stillness that recalls Vermeer's domestic scenes.*

School of Campin The Mérode Altarpiece St Joseph c.1425
(right) *The right-hand wing of this Flemish altarpiece shows St Joseph in his carpenter's shop; a 15th-century Netherlandish town can be glimpsed through the window.*

Cloisters Collection, 1956/Metropolitan Museum of Art, N.Y.

considerable vogue in the 18th century, although it was well known before then. There are two main features of Vermeer's work that point towards the use of a camera obscura. The first is his exaggerated perspective, in which figures and objects in the foreground seem to loom very large compared with the others further back. Anyone who has used a wide-angle lens on a camera will know that this is just the effect they can create. The second indication is the way in which certain parts of Vermeer's paintings – particularly sparkling highlights – often look fuzzy or out of focus: again this is exactly what one would expect to happen with the primitive lenses then in use.

After Vermeer's death, the biologist Anthony van Leeuwenhoeck, who later became famous for his work with microscopes, was appointed trustee of his estate. There is no other indication that the great painter and the great scientist knew each other, but a common interest in optics could well have brought them together. As with so much to do with Vermeer, there is wide scope for speculation as the facts of the matter remain intriguingly elusive.

National Gallery, London

TRADEMARKS
Pictures within Pictures

The pictures that appear in the background of many of Vermeer's paintings usually have a symbolic meaning which would have been readily understood by his contemporaries. Several of the pictures themselves were once owned by the Vermeer family.

Lady Standing at the Virginals
(above and right) The meaning of this work is implicit in the painting hanging on the wall, showing Cupid, the god of love, holding up a playing card. Such images were described in detail in emblem books of the time, as symbols of fidelity – often with the motto 'Only One'. Vermeer's painting may allude to the relationship between true love and musical harmony. The woman's gentle radiance and quietly confident gaze seems to reinforce this interpretation.

THE MAKING OF A MASTERPIECE

The Artist's Studio

This allegory on the art of painting, popularly known as *The Artist's Studio*, shows an artist in historical dress painting a portrait of Clio, the Muse of History. The inclusion of a map of the Netherlands on the back wall implies that the allegory refers specifically to Netherlandish painting, and it may be that Vermeer was seeking to emphasize the importance of history painting in the art of his country. Nothing is known for certain about the circumstances in which the picture was painted, but it is possible that Vermeer intended it as a gift to the Delft Guild of St Luke, of which he was an officer. At around the time he was painting the picture, the Guild was having new headquarters built on the Voldegracht behind Vermeer's house. The building was adorned with statues and paintings of the liberal arts, so a picture like this, with its complex symbolism, would have been in keeping with the rest of the decoration. Vermeer, however, was so attached to this work that he kept it until his death in 1675.

Kunsthistorisches Museum, Vienna

Artothek

Curtain onto another world
(left) A richly-coloured tapestry falls in heavy folds across the left-hand side of the composition. It is drawn aside to usher us into the artificial space of the picture.

Allegory of Faith
(right) For his second and more overtly allegorical painting, Vermeer referred to the same handbook that he used for The Artist's Studio: *Cesare Ripa's Iconologia. From this source he borrowed various symbolic details like the chalice, the crown of thorns, the apple and the snake.*

Bequest of Michael Friedsam, 1931

Metropolitan Museum, N.Y.

Lauros-Giraudon

Louvre, Paris

Symbolic attributes
(left) In Le Sueur's painting of the muses, Clio (on the left) is given the same attributes as Vermeer's muse – both artists used Ripa's manual, then an extremely popular source-book.

Points of light
(below) Vermeer's so-called pointillé technique is seen in the gleaming chandelier, where the highlights on the bronze are meticulously suggested by splotches or dots of paint.

'A certain piece of Painting in which is represented the Art of Painting.'

Vermeer's mother-in-law

Historical costume
(left) Vermeer has represented the artist in late medieval costume, so that he would have been recognized by a 17th-century observer as an 'old master'. The muse, Clio, is shown exactly according to the description in Ripa: 'a maiden with a laurel garland who holds a trumpet in her right hand and with her left a book.' These 'antique' details suggest that Vermeer's allegory is inspired by his veneration of history painting, the highest profession. Clio, the muse of History – holding a trumpet symbolizing fame – is about to be immortalized.

Gallery

Most of Vermeer's paintings are small – even tiny – in scale and involve only one or two figures engaged in some unremarkable domestic activity. Sometimes there is the suggestion of a concealed meaning, as in The Music Lesson and The Concert, and occasionally Vermeer painted a more elaborate piece, such as The Artist's Studio,

The Glass of Wine *c.1658-60*
25″ × 30″ Staatliche Museen, West Berlin

This painting has many of the characteristics we think of as typical of Vermeer's works: a single source of light on the left, a chair placed at a three-quarter angle to the viewer, an elaborate carpet on the table, a picture on an otherwise bare wall and quiet figures absorbed in an everyday activity.

but essentially the impact of Vermeer's work rests not on what he portrays but on how he portrays it.

The spellbinding beauty of his paintings depends very much on his sensitivity to light and his flawless technique, every pinpoint of light rendered with unerring sureness in works such as The Lacemaker or The Guitar Player. Astonishingly, Vermeer could transfer this optical subtlety from the intimacy of his studio to the outside world. The Little Street is one of his most charming works and in the View of Delft he created an unparalleled masterpiece that combines complete unity of atmosphere with exquisite perfection of detail.

Soldier with a Laughing Girl *c.1658-60*
19¾″ × 18″ Frick Collection, New York

Until 1866, when it was identified by Theophile Thoré in a private collection in Paris, this picture was attributed to Pieter de Hooch. Fifteen years later it was sold for 88,000 francs, then an enormous sum, an indication of how much Thoré's work had done to establish Vermeer's reputation.

The Little Street *c.1660*
21¼″ × 17″ Rijksmuseum, Amsterdam

Vermeer's two landscape paintings are his most original works, for in them he seems to look with an utterly fresh eye and without any sense of contrivance. This picture is particularly loved in Holland, where it is called simply the 'Straatje' (the Street). The blue-looking foliage has been caused by fading of yellow from the green.

View of Delft *c.1660*
38″ × 46″ Mauritshuis, The Hague

Holland produced many outstanding landscape painters in the 17th century, but in his one excursion into their territory Vermeer produced a work that surpassed even their greatest masterpieces in lucidity and truth to life. The atmosphere of an overcast day is caught perfectly, as the sun breaks through the heavy clouds to light up the distant roofs.

The Music Lesson *c.1660-65*
28″ × 35″ Royal Collection

The inscription on the lid of the virginals reads Musica Letitiae
Comes Medicina Doloris *(Music is the companion of joy and the
balm of sorrow) and it has been suggested that rather than being the
woman's teacher, the man is in fact paying court to her. Vermeer,
however, subtly refrains from making anything explicit.*

The Concert *c.1660-65*
27¼″ × 24¾″ Isabella Stewart Gardner Museum, Boston

The right-hand painting on the wall behind the three figures is The
Procuress *by Dirck van Baburen (p.111); it appears in another of
Vermeer's works and it seems that his mother-in-law owned it. The
sexual subject hints that stronger passions may lurk behind the quiet
exteriors of Vermeer's figures.*

Meyer/Artothek

The Artist's Studio *c.1665-70*
51″ × 43¾″ Kunsthistorisches Museum, Vienna

*It is often suggested that Vermeer has here represented himself at work
and it would be apposite for an artist about whom so little is known to
produce such a teasingly enigmatic self-portrait. Adolf Hitler seized
this painting from the family that owned it and it was among a horde
of such works recovered from an Austrian salt mine in 1945.*

The Love Letter *c.1670*
17½″ × 15¼″ Rijksmuseum, Amsterdam

*The 'dramatic' features of this work – the rather exaggerated sense of
movement into depth and the strong lighting in the background –
suggest a late date, when Vermeer was moving away from the serene
simplicity of his most characteristic works. In 1971 this picture was
stolen while on exhibition in Brussels and seriously damaged.*

The Geographer *1669*
20″ × 18¼″ Städelsches Kunstinstitut, Frankfurt

Apart from the early Procuress *(p.112), this and the painting opposite are the only works by Vermeer that bear a date. The Geographer and The Astronomer were painted as a pair and remained together until 1797. Vermeer has shown the geographer pausing for thought as he looks up from his work.*

The Astronomer *1668*
19¾″ × 18″ Private Collection

*Pictures of scholars in their studies were popular in 17th-century
Holland – Rembrandt, for example, made several. However, whereas
Rembrandt usually gives his figures a mystical quality, Vermeer's
astronomer and geographer are engaged in deep but rational thought.
Vermeer's works suggest that he, too, had a mind that loved clarity.*

Bridgeman Art Library

The Lacemaker *c.1670*
9¼″ × 8″ Louvre, Paris

*This tiny painting is one of Vermeer's loveliest creations. Needlework
was a traditional symbol of modest homeliness, but the tenderness and
intimacy of the portrayal, together with the extraordinarily beautiful
handling of light, transcend any feeling of the commonplace. Renoir
said that he considered this one of the finest paintings in the world.*

The Guitar Player *c.1670-75*
20″ × 18″ Kenwood, London

*The sense of luxury in this painting – in the woman's obviously
expensive clothes, for example – probably reflects the French influence
that was making itself felt in Dutch painting at this time. Many critics
see in this greater sophistication a weakening of Vermeer's powers, but
none deny the beauty with which the rich materials are painted.*

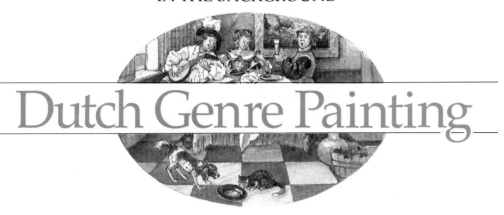

Dutch Genre Painting

**Although its roots were in the early 16th century, genre painting
really came into its own in the newly independent Dutch lands in the
early to middle parts of the 17th century.**

Merry Company
*(below) This picture,
entitled* Merry
Company in the Open
Air, *painted c.1616-17 by
Willem Buytewech,
records the carefree
pleasures of his
generation, enjoying the
boom time that came with
the ending of wars and
the foundation of the
Dutch Republic.*

In April 1609, the Spanish Empire signed a 12-year truce with the Netherlands, formally recognizing the United Provinces as an independent commonwealth. This event was to have important consequences for the development of Dutch art. The first few decades of the 17th century witnessed a new prosperity, and the independent nation quickly achieved outstanding commercial success. This fostered the emergence of an unusually large and wealthy middle-class and these prosperous citizens were enthusiastic 'consumers' of art. The English traveller Peter Mundy visited Amsterdam in 1640 and commented on the Dutchman's

enthusiasm for paintings: 'As for the art off Painting and the affection off the people to Pictures, I thincke none other goe beeyond them . . . All in generall striving to adorne their houses, especially the outer or streete roome, with costly peeces . . .' Also, in 1641 John Evelyn visited Rotterdam and was amazed at the number of pictures being hawked at the Fair, 'especially Landskips, and Drolleries'.

As Evelyn remarked, the enthusiasm of this art-buying public was primarily for 'Drolleries', or genre paintings, as they are now known. These are scenes of everyday, contemporary life. The

Adriaen Brouwer; Pancake Baker

The Pancake Baker
(left) *A scene of coarse peasant reality. An innovation when it was painted in the mid-1620s, Adriaen Brouwer's work depicts an everyday scene from lower-class life with biting accuracy.*

Saying Grace
(right) *Nicholas Maes' scene of simple piety painted c.1655 was the type of image that a well-ordered and pious Dutch family would see as an example to follow.*

Mercenary love
(below) *Gerard Terborch's* A Soldier Offering a Young Woman Coins *shows a girl's indecision about immorality but the theme is almost lost if the sumptuousness of her attire is contemplated.*

N. Maes; Saying Grace/Rijksmuseum, Amsterdam

'consumers' were not much interested in devotional paintings or altarpieces, which had little place in the austere buildings of the Dutch Reformed Church. Nor did they share the Italian patron's enthusiasm for paintings of historical and mythological scenes. They were interested in paintings which showed themselves and their surroundings and depicted the events, the shapes and the colours of everyday life.

Genre painting did not, however, originate with the signing of the 12-year truce, although it undeniably flourished under the new economic and social conditions. It had its roots in the art of

the early 16th century, particularly in the moralizing paintings of Hieronymous Bosch and Pieter Bruegel the Elder. Both Bosch and Bruegel had painted scenes from everyday life, using the activities of ordinary folk in an allegorical way: to illustrate the vices, to point out a moral lesson or to illustrate a proverb. Bruegel had amused his well-to-do patrons with vivid scenes of peasant revelry – using the example of peasant debauchery to illustrate the dangers of gluttony and lust. Genre painters of the 17th century, such as Adriaen Brouwer, repeatedly took up this theme, producing numerous (different) scenes of peasants at play, often with a moral implied.

The more socially elevated equivalent of this theme was the popular *Merry Company* (opposite), which had its origins in 16th-century religious and mythological paintings. Paintings of the Marriage at Cana, the Feasting of the Prodigal Son, or Mankind Feasting Before the Flood, offered numerous precedents for the depiction of elegant revellers disporting themselves. These too had moral overtones, pointing out that the pleasures of the senses lead to sin and destruction. Genre painters of the 17th century transposed these themes into their own times, dressing their revellers in contemporary costume and placing them in inns and taverns. Here, they drink smoke and make music as a prelude to more intimate sensual pleasures. During the early years of the century, the moralizing tradition behind these pictures must have seemed particularly

Jan Steen; The Doctor's Visit/Mauritshuis, The Hague

A medical consultation

(above) In Jan Steen's The Doctor's Visit, a love-sick (possibly pregnant) young girl lounges in bed. The painting is packed with clues to the theme and the antics of the dogs and the goings on in the painting on the wall behind the bed leave little to the imagination.

Woman Reading a Letter

(below) This is the companion painting to Gabriel Metsu's Man Writing a Letter. In this second part of the amorous narrative, the theme is underscored by the servant exposing a stormy scene, no doubt to emphasize the turbulence of the emotion of love.

Metsu; Woman Reading a Letter/Sir Alfred Beit Foundation

appropriate, as the 'nouveaux riches' of Dutch society flaunted and squandered their new-found wealth.

Also at the beginning of the century, genre painters confined themselves largely to variations on these two themes: low-life debauchery and high-life 'merry companies'. As the century wore on, however, the range of genre painting expanded rapidly to include guard-room scenes with soldiers at rest or play, brothel scenes, intimate domestic interiors and illustrations of doctors or craftsmen at work. Painters often confined themselves to one small branch of genre, developing a specialization which seemed to promise a secure market.

With this proliferation of types and subjects, the moral and allegorical aspects of genre painting became less pronounced. The genre paintings of the second half of the century should be seen, first and foremost, as depictions of contemporary life. The owner of a genre painting appreciated it primarily as a mirror of his own environment, and of his own cultural values. Nicholas Maes' painting of Saying Grace (p.133) may, for example, have moralizing overtones but it is also a simple illustration of piety and domestic order, qualities which the 17th-century Dutchman particularly prized. Terborch's painting of A Soldier Offering a Young Woman Coins (p.133) deals with the common theme of mercenary love, yet the moral aspect of the subject is of secondary interest beside the vivid portrayal of the girl's indecision and the meticulous rendering of her dress.

FOLLY SATIRIZED

On occasion, however, a genre painter could still take a sternly moralizing tone. Jan Steen, for example, specialized in comic low-life scenes in the tradition of Pieter Bruegel. Using contemporary events, such as a Christening or a wedding feast, Steen satirized the folly and debauchery of common folk with a clear moral intention. In his smaller domestic scenes, Steen made abundant and obvious use of symbolism to point a finger at contemporary vice. In the Doctor's Visit (this page), for instance, a young woman languishes, ill with love-sickness. The nature of her illness is made clear by the actions of the dogs in the doorway, which are obvious symbols of licentiousness. Behind her, the picture on the wall shows a scene of pagan revelry which continues the theme of unbridled lust.

Some genre painters chose to specialize in paintings depicting the professions. These paintings provide a compelling record of 17th-century life, as here, the professionals and the artisans are shown surrounded by the tools of their trade, painted with minute attention to detail. In The Baker (opposite), for example, he is surrounded by different types of bread and in the background are a baker's utensils. The stone archway behind him is appropriate for a baker's shop since, from the early 16th century, bakers had been forbidden

The Baker

(right) A common theme of the genre painters was the depiction of trades or professions. This painting, painted c.1681 by Job Berckhyde, not only shows the baker surrounded by his wares and tools but also has sexual overtones in the man blowing his horn to announce that he is ready to sell his bread.

Courtyard in Delft

(below) A woman and child pause on some steps by the doorway of the courtyard. A more straightforward example of genre painting would be hard to find than this by Pieter de Hooch.

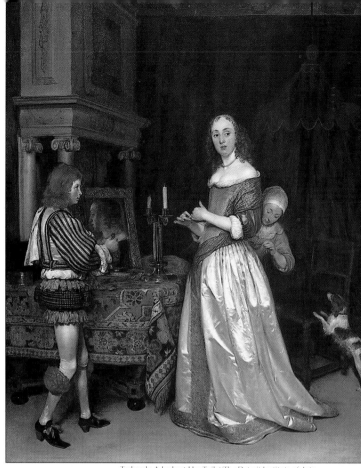

to light ovens in wooden houses. He blows his horn to announce the morning's bread, an action which may also have sexual overtones.

One of the most talented genre painters of the second half of the century was the Delft painter Pieter de Hooch, Vermeer's predecessor. Like many genre artists de Hooch painted refined 'merry company' scenes; he also painted smaller groups of men and women drinking together, in interiors or in courtyards, which often carry sexual overtones. But his most important contribution was in paintings of domestic scenes. De Hooch made a particular art out of painting scenes of middle-class home life, where soberly dressed women quietly carry out their domestic chores. He also had an unparalleled grasp of perspective and located his figures in perfectly constructed interiors, whose symmetry and order seem to reflect the virtue and harmony of their occupants. These neat, orderly interiors provide a telling illustration of the ideals and values of the Dutch middle-class.

De Hooch's paintings also make it clear that, for contemporary purchasers, the beauty of genre paintings lay largely in their realism, and their minute attention to the colours, shapes and textures of everyday life. The charm of de Hooch's paintings lies primarily in his meticulous depiction of space and light, and his awareness of the shapes of objects half-concealed in a dim interior.

Despite the diversity of their subject-matter, genre painters were unfailingly realistic, focusing with unusual precision on the surface of a silk dress, the reflection of light on a jug, or the texture of a Turkish carpet. Few painters surpassed Vermeer in this respect. In his serene, orderly interiors, which perfect the innovations of de Hooch, Vermeer managed to raise to new heights the art of the everyday.

Lady at Her Toilet
(above) Gerard Terborch's woman taking off her jewellery, painted c.1660, is a lush look at the elegance of a wealthy lifestyle. The sensuousness of the furnishings and clothing enhances the idea that the woman, removing her ring prior to washing her hands, is performing the act to atone for some perhaps regretted amorous adventure.

135

A Year in 1654
the Life

The great explosion at Vermeer's native Delft was only one of several sensations during 1654 but the event that set all Europe talking was the abdication of Sweden's gifted and eccentric Queen Christina. Monarchy was by divine right and not to be trifled with as Louis XIV, crowned during this year, was to prove.

For the Netherlands as a whole 1654 was a year of setbacks. Over the previous quarter of a century the Dutch had struggled to establish trading colonies in Brazil, thus supplanting Portuguese interests but the Dutch West India Company had made itself unpopular by exploitation and high-handedness. This resulted in a revolt which with Portuguese help succeeded in permanently ousting Dutch trading interests from Brazil.

A second blow was the Anglo-Dutch Treaty of Westminster. This ended a war which had gone badly for the Dutch, who were forced to make unpalatable public concessions to the English Commonwealth under its new Lord Protector, Oliver Cromwell. Secret treaty arrangements were also made that became known and caused a public outcry, since they involved English interference with Dutch internal affairs. The Act of

E. P. Goldschmidt & Co. Ltd/Ann Ronan Picture Library

Mauro Pucciarelli

Prado, Madrid

Magdeburg Hemispheres
(above) Legend has it that on 8 May 1654, Otto von Guericke of Magdeburg amazed the Holy Roman Emperor and the assembled Reichstag by a demonstration of the power of air pressure at Regensburg. Two teams of eight horses could not pull apart two halves of an evacuated copper sphere.

Swedish adventuress
(left) Queen Christina's unprecedented decision to abdicate in 1654 was mainly due to her wish to convert to Catholicism, a criminal offence in Sweden. Drawn to settle in Rome, she soon became a leading figure in social and cultural circles, despite her headstrong nature and renowned eccentricity as expressed by a liking for male clothing and her liaison with a Roman Cardinal.

Seclusion banned the eminent Orange family who were to be kept out of power because of their links with the exiled English royal family, the Stuarts. By a strange irony, the four-year-old William of Orange would eventually become ruler of both England and the Netherlands 35 years later.

AN EXTRAORDINARY WOMAN

By contrast with the makeshifts of diplomacy, the abdication of Sweden's Queen Christina was an irrevocable act – and something of a scandal in an age when rulers were regarded as divinely chosen beings who would do their duty whatever their personal inclinations. A gifted woman who had made her court a splendid cultural centre, Christina was also unstable and

wildly extravagant. Her abdication was partly a flight from difficult political problems and partly a religious impulse (she was about to convert to Catholicism, a faith no Swedish monarch was allowed to profess).

Before the end of the year Christina, while in Brussels, had made a secret conversion to Catholicism which was publicly celebrated with booming cannon and firework displays the following year. She was to settle in Rome where her constant financial difficulties encouraged a revival of her political ambitions, frequently interfering in Vatican politics and international affairs. After throwing away one crown, she indulged in long and futile intrigues to become Queen of Naples and later, Poland. Despite often making herself ridiculous she was a powerful cultural influence in Rome until

Dutch lose Brazil

(right) This idyllic view of a Dutch colonial settlement in Brazil is by Frans Post who accompanied the Dutch West India Company's voyage of colonization (1637-44). However, by 1654 the experiment was over. Portugal, united under the same monarchy with Spain between 1580 and 1640, was furious at the way Spain had allowed the Dutch to take control of her prized colony and eventually reclaimed Brazil.

Franz Post/Dutch colonist house in Brazil/Rijksmuseum, Amsterdam

Pascal retires

(left) Blaise Pascal, the French mathematician and theologian, retired to the Jansenist convent of Port-Royal at the close of 1654, aged 31. The nine-year struggle between his commitment to scientific discovery, eventually seen as the product of self-love, and his spiritual well-being was over.

Tsar Alexei

(right) In 1654 a famous bargain was struck between the Cossacks under their **Hetman** Chmielnicki and the Romanov Tsar Alexei by which the former agreed to accept unconditionally the latter's authority in perpetuity. The Cossacks could now act in concert with Moscow against Poland.

Bulloz

Collection Ulysse Moussolli

Michael Holford

Countess Bobrinskoy Collection

her death in 1689. The composers Corelli and Scarlatti were attached to her household and the Baroque architect and sculptor Bernini was counted an intimate friend.

In the same year as Sweden gained a new monarch in Charles X, cousin to the extraordinary Christina, the 16-year-old Louis XIV was officially consecrated King of France at Rheims Cathedral. Louis bided his time until Mazarin's death in 1661 before taking the reins of government entirely into his own hands. He created a personalised autocracy which, with his single-minded pursuit of *gloire*, would be the wonder of the age. In 1654 France was still racked by Civil War with the Prince de Condé fighting his erstwhile *Frondeur* ally, Marshall Turenne. However, Louis had the satisfaction of witnessing the latter relieve the town of Arras under siege by the Great Condé.

Meanwhile on the margins of civilized Europe, the Cossacks of the Ukraine had responded to the call of their *Hetman*, or leader Chmielnicki, to rebel against their Polish oppressors. Now, unable to maintain complete independence without backing, they chose a new master.

Finally, a spectacular series of experiments publicized the work of Otto von Guericke, a German scientist who had already invented the air pump and used it to prove that while light can travel through a vacuum sound cannot. It was thought that at Regensburg, in 1654, in the presence of the Emperor Ferdinand III, horses straining in different directions failed to pull apart two copper bowls, enclosing a vacuum, which were placed edge to edge to form a sphere. Sheer air pressure was proved strong enough to defeat horse power.

Réunion des Musées Nationaux

Versailles

The Lord's anointed
(left) Louis XIV had succeeded to his father's throne in 1643 at the tender age of four years and eight months. His mother, Anne of Austria, acted as Regent until Louis' thirteenth year when he officially took over the reins of government. He was finally anointed King of France in a splendid ceremony at Rheims Cathedral in 1654 but did not assume real control until the death of the First Minister, Cardinal Mazarin in 1661. No successor was appointed and the young King began 54 years of absolute rule. From this time onwards he could in truth declare; 'L'État, c'est moi'.

Grand Pensionary
(right) The death of William II, Prince of Orange, in 1650 led to the first 'Stadholderless period' whereby the United Provinces were ruled by a Grand Pensionary or chief officer of the province of Holland. The new régime, which upheld republicanism, was against the centralist policies of the House of Orange. It was thus to their advantage to agree to exclude the Orange family from high office as part of the Anglo-Dutch peace of 1654.

Mansell Collection

GALLERY GUIDE

Rubens

Rubens was a prolific artist; most major European and American galleries own examples of his work. In his home town of Antwerp, there are paintings in the Musée Royal des Beaux-Arts and the Rubenshuis, while Antwerp Cathedral houses The Raising of the Cross and The Descent from the Cross (pp.24-5). There are also altarpieces in the Augustinuskerk, the St Jacobskerk and the St Pauluskerk – all churches in Antwerp. Rubens' commission from the French monarchy – the 25 paintings in the Marie de' Medici cycle (pp.30-31) – are housed in the Louvre in Paris, along with several other works. The National Gallery in London owns Rubens' famous Chapeau de Paille (p.29) and many landscapes; in the nearby Whitehall Banqueting House the ceiling depicting an allegory on the reign of James I (p.16) is still in situ. The Kunsthistorisches Museum in Vienna houses an excellent collection, including Helena Fourment as Venus and the Alte Pinakothek in Munich contains The Abduction of the Daughters of Leucippus and The Last Judgement. In America, fine works by Rubens can be seen in the Metropolitan Museum of Art, New York, The National Gallery of Art, Washington, and Philadelphia Museum of Art.

Hals

The Frans Halsmuseum in Haarlem contains the best single collection of his work. The Rijksmuseum in Amsterdam also owns several well-known paintings but his most famous painting, The Laughing Cavalier (p.57), is in the Wallace Collection in London. In Paris, the Louvre has a good collection that includes The Gypsy Girl (p.62), and the Berlin-Dahlem Staatliche Museen owns Malle Babbe (p.63). In America, works by Hals can be seen in the Taft Museum, Cincinnati, the National Gallery of Art, Washington, and the Metropolitan Museum of Art, New York, which has Shrovetide Revellers (p.50) among others.

Rembrandt

There are good examples of Rembrandt's work in many Dutch museums including the Rijksmuseum in Amsterdam, which houses two of his most famous pictures, The Night Watch (pp.92-3) and The Jewish Bride (p.99), and the Mauritshuis in The Hague, which owns Saul and David. Elsewhere in Europe, Rembrandts can be seen in Dresden (Gemaldegalerie), Berlin (Berlin-Dahlem Staatliche Museen), Brunswick (Herzog Anton Ulrich Museum), Kassel (Staatliche Gemaldegalerie), Munich (Alte Pinakothek), Vienna (Kunsthistorisches Museum) and the Louvre in Paris. The National Gallery in London owns a particularly fine collection of Rembrandts which includes A Woman Bathing in a Stream (p.96) and Saskia as Flora (p.91). The Hermitage in Leningrad has an excellent, if less well-known, selection of pictures by Rembrandt. The best examples of Rembrandt's work in America are to be found in The Metropolitan Museum, New York, and in the Frick Collection, also in New York, which owns the enigmatic Polish Rider.

Vermeer

There are only about 35 known paintings by Vermeer, so his works are quite rare. The famous View of Delft (p.123) can be seen in the Mauritshuis in The Hague, while the Rijksmuseum in Amsterdam houses the well-known Maid with a Milk Jug (p.115) and The Little Street (p.122), along with several other pictures. The painter's enigmatic The Artist's Studio (p.126) can be seen in the Kunsthistorisches Museum in Vienna, and elsewhere in Europe there are fine works in London (National Gallery), Dresden (Gemaldegalerie) and Berlin (Berlin-Dahlem Staatliche Museen). The Frick Collection and the Metropolitan Museum, both in New York, and the Isabella Stewart Gardner Museum in Boston, all have Vermeers. A Woman Weighing Pearls is housed in the National Gallery of Art, Washington.

BIBLIOGRAPHY

H. P. Baard, Hals, Abrams, New York, 1981
A. Blankert, Vermeer of Delft, Phaidon, Oxford, 1978
P. Cabanne, Rubens, Thames and Hudson, London, 1968
K. Clarke, An Introduction to Rembrandt, Harper & Row, New York, 1978
K. Downes, Rubens, Hipprocrene Books, New York, 1984
E. Gerson and E. H. ter Kuile, Art and Architecture in Belgium, Viking Books, New York, 1978
M. Kitson, Rembrandt, Merrimack Publishers

Circle, Salem, 1983
I. J. Slatkes, Vermeer and his Contemporaries, Abbeville Press, New York, 1981
C. White, Rembrandt, Thames and Hudson, London, 1984
C. White, Rubens and his World, Thames and Hudson, London, 1968
C. Wright, The Dutch Painters: 100 Seventeenth Century Masters, Barron, Woodbury, 1978
C. Wright, Vermeer, Hipprocrene Books, New York, 1977

Adriaen Brouwer (1605/6-1638)

Born in Oudenaarde in Flanders, Brouwer spent part of his brief and apparently dissolute life working in Haarlem, where he may have studied with Frans Hals. Brouwer refashioned the Breughel tradition of peasant painting to produce several humorous genre scenes of oafish-looking men carousing and brawling in taverns, executed in a dashing and vigorous style. In The Smokers (Metropolitan Museum, New York) the artist even showed himself and his painter friends indulging in an orgy of merrymaking. Brouwer's pictures helped initiate low-life genre painting in Holland, thus providing an important link between the Dutch and Flemish schools of painting.

Gerard (Gerrit) Dou (1613-1675)

Gerrit Dou trained with Rembrandt in Leiden, and even collaborated with him on the picture Anna and the Blind Tobit in the National Gallery, London. Perhaps because of Rembrandt's overwhelming presence, Dou only arrived at his mature style after his master had left Leiden for Amsterdam. He then began to produce small, highly-finished genre paintings full of such minute detail that he sometimes needed the aid of a magnifying glass while he worked. It was this meticulous technique that was to form the basis of the Leiden school of fijnschilders (fine painters). Dou rarely left his native Leiden, but he achieved an international reputation, with patrons that included Charles II of England and Queen Christina of

Two Kinds of Games (below) Like many of Jan Steen's paintings, this lively tavern scene contains an implied attack on debauchery: while the three players concentrate on their game, the elderly customer tries to seduce an unwilling serving girl.

Sweden. There are works by Dou in many European galleries – the most notable examples being in Amsterdam (Rijksmuseum), Dresden (Gemaldegalerie), Leningrad (The Hermitage), Munich (Alte Pinakothek), and London (Dulwich Picture Gallery).

Gerrit van Honthorst (1590-1656)

Honthorst was born in Utrecht, but he is said to have been in Rome by about 1610, where he enjoyed the patronage of notable collectors such as Cardinal Scipione Borghese, and established a reputation as one of the city's foremost painters. The nickname that Honthorst acquired in Italy – Gerardo delle Notte – (Gerard of the night scenes) – points to the fact that his fame was founded on his nocturnal pictures. The inspiration behind these was partly derived from the Italian painter Caravaggio, and Honthorst was instrumental in awakening interest in the Caravaggesque style of painting, with its exaggerated tonal contrasts and gestures, in his native Utrecht. However, on his return to the Netherlands, Honthorst turned away from Biblical scenes and night pictures and began to paint light-hearted scenes using a brighter palette. Honthorst's later work was highly prized during his lifetime, and Charles I even invited the artist to England to paint his portrait (now in the National Portrait Gallery, London). Modern taste, however, tends to prefer the early pictures in the galleries and churches of Rome.

Pieter de Hooch (1629-1684)

Vermeer's great contemporary in Delft, Pieter de Hooch, shared his fascination with the fall of light in an interior, and his delight in the tranquil moments of domestic life. Which artist was the first to develop these quiet subjects in painting has long been a matter for debate, but it appears that de Hooch was producing scenes of men and women in sunlit courtyards and ordered interiors a few years before Vermeer. Until 1660, de Hooch produced pictures of great charm and simplicity, but his move to Amsterdam in that year seems to have prompted him to experiment with a more ornate style of painting in which the interiors are rather more ostentatious than before, and the tonality is noticeably darker. There are good de Hoochs in Amsterdam (Rijksmuseum), Berlin (Nationalgalerie), London (National Gallery and Wallace Collection), Paris (Louvre), and Washington (National Gallery of Art).

Jacob Jordaens (1593-1678)

The leading painter in Flanders after the death of Rubens, Jordaens produced a vast number of altarpieces, genre pictures, portraits and mythological scenes, as well as etchings and tapestry designs. Although he had his own workshop in Antwerp, he assisted Rubens with many commissions, including the paintings for Philip IV's hunting lodge in Madrid, the Torre de la Prada. Jordaen's work shows the influence of Rubens'

Rijksmuseum, Amsterdam

flamboyant style, but he tended to use thicker impasto and more pronounced chiaroscuro. During his later years, following his conversion to Calvinism, Jordaens' colours became more subdued. Jordaens was one of a group of artists that included Rembrandt and Jan Lievens, who were chosen to decorate the Town Hall in Amsterdam, but his best known pictures can be seen in various churches in Antwerp.

Nicholas Maes (1634-1693)

One of Rembrandt's pupils, Nicholas Maes began his career as a painter of genre scenes, many of which show housewives or maids engaged in domestic pursuits such as sewing, preparing food, spinning, falling asleep, idly dreaming, or eavesdropping on other people's conversations. These pictures, with their subtle moods and delicate tones, are quiet masterpieces in their own way, and no convincing reason has yet been advanced to explain why the artist gave up painting them around 1660 to concentrate exclusively on portraiture. Paintings by Maes can be seen in most European galleries.

Gabriel Metsu (1629-1667)

Born in Leiden, Metsu was reputedly apprenticed to Gerrit Dou and trained in the tradition of 'fine painting', although his meticulous, delicate style did not fully develop until he settled in Amsterdam in 1657. The artist specialized in bourgeois interiors, music parties, brothel scenes and pictures of men and women going about their daily tasks. His works resemble de Hooch and Vermeer in their subject matter and approach, but Metsu's tonal contrasts are more subdued than de Hooch's, and the edges of his forms are softer and the paint thinner than in Vermeer. Metsu's best-known pictures are The Music Lesson (National Gallery, London) and The Sick Child (Rijksmuseum, Amsterdam).

Pieter Saenredam (1597-1665)

A hunchback recluse who spent his life in Haarlem, Saenredam specialized in architectural views of specific buildings, painting both interiors and exteriors. He recorded churches, halls and galleries in minute detail, working out perspective with mathematical precision. Yet Saenredam's works are more than just tinted architectural drawings, as the artist was acutely sensitive to the fleeting movements of light and shadow across a façade, and his carefully placed clusters of people always add humanity to the bare, whitewashed interiors of Calvinist churches and Dutch streets. Saenredam worked slowly, and there are only about 50 known works by him in existence, the best examples of which are in Dutch museums.

Frans Snyders (1597-1657)

A pupil of Pieter Breughel the Younger, Frans Snyders spent most of his life working in his native Antwerp, apart from a short visit to Italy. He made his reputation as a painter of animals, robust hunting scenes, markets and elaborate cornucopian still-lifes. Snyders worked for a while in Rubens' studio, and collaborated with him on a number of his great canvases, usually painting in details such as animals, flowers and fruit. His works may be seen in Antwerp (Musée Royal des Beaux-Arts) and Leningrad (The Hermitage).

Jan Steen (1625/6-1679)

A native of Leiden, Jan Steen produced a large number of humorous genre scenes showing chaotic households, quack doctors visiting lovesick girls, and general merrymaking. Although his pictures display great comic talent, they often contain an implied condemnation of debauchery, and many illustrate well-known Dutch proverbs. There is no certain factual basis for the romantic image of Steen as a drunken profligate of the type portrayed in his paintings, even though he did own a tavern in Delft at one point. Steen also painted several serious religious and mythological paintings, but these are less famous than his genre scenes. Over 800 pictures by Steen are known to exist, and he is well represented in European and American museums, the best examples of his work being found in The Hague (Mauritshuis), Leningrad (The Hermitage), London (Wallace Collection) and Rotterdam (Museum Boymans-van Beuningen).

David Teniers the Younger (1610-1690)

A highly prolific Flemish artist who was born in Antwerp and worked there and in Brussels, Teniers' fame rests upon his peasant scenes which were derived from the work of Adriaen Brouwer, but were given a more elegant and refined treatment. In 1651 Teniers was appointed court painter to Archduke Leopold Wilhelm in Brussels. One of his tasks in this post was to look after the Archduke's superb collection of pictures, and he painted several views of the gallery in which it was housed, as well as making many copies of the paintings themselves. These pictures can be seen in the Kunsthistorisches Museum in Vienna, the Musée Royal des Beaux Arts, Brussels, and the Prado, Madrid.

Gerard Terborch (1617-81)

Terborch is chiefly remembered as a painter of intimate interiors featuring elegant women in sumptuous silks, satins and velvets, at their toilet or in conversation with men. The gentility of atmosphere in these paintings sometimes disguises the fact that these are brothel scenes, the best-known example of which is the so-called Parental Admonition in Berlin (Berlin-Dahlem Staatliche Museen). The picture's title derives from the fact that it was thought for years to be a depiction of a father rebuking his daughter, rather than a man offering money to a prostitute. Terborch also produced moving vignettes of quite mundane events, such as boys removing fleas from dogs, women preparing meals, and mothers combing their children's hair. The artist's best paintings can be seen in Amsterdam (Rijksmuseum), Berlin (Berlin-Dahlem Staatliche Museen), London (National Gallery), and Munich (Alte Pinakothek).

Willem van der Velde the Younger (1633-1707)

The most famous member of a family of distinguished marine artists, Willem van der Velde the Younger is also the most highly regarded of all Dutch painters of the sea. He always took great pains to ensure that every detail of sail, mast and rigging was correct in his pictures, but his art was never pedantic or dull. The compositions all possess a certain majesty and drama, whether they show ships in a calm, caught up in a storm, or in the midst of battle. Many of the finest van der Veldes can be seen at the National Maritime Museum in Greenwich, London.